Pregnancy chic

Pregnancy chic

The fashion survival guide

Cherie Serota and Jody Kozlow Gardner

Illustrations by Tracey Wood

A Balliett & Fitzgerald Book

Villard

New York

To my husband, Daniel, who spoils me with
unyielding love and understanding; to my very
special parents, who have taught me that you can
do anything in life you set your mind to; and to
my two adorable sons, Stephen and Jonathan, who
bring a smile to my face and laughter to my heart.
C.S.

This book is dedicated to my parents, who taught
me to never give up and made me what I am
today; to David, my soul mate and life's guide; and
to Jade and Grant, who every day teach me the
true meaning of joy.
J.K.G.

With special thanks to Michael Gould and Liz Bailey for making it happen.

—◦⁄∕◦—

All rights reserved under International and Pan-American Copyright Conventions. Published in the United
States by Villard Books, a division of Random House, Inc., New York, and simultaneously in Canada by
Random House of Canada Limited, Toronto.

VILLARD BOOKS is a registered trademark of Random House, Inc.

Belly Basics™ is a registered trademark.

Library of Congress Cataloging-in-Publication Data
Pregnancy chic: the fashion survival guide / Cherie Serota and Jody Kozlow Gardner
        p.   cm.
    ISBN 0-375-50027-8
    1. Maternity clothes.   I. Gardner, Jody Kozlow.   II. Title.
    TT547.S47   1998
646.4′04—dc21   97-36474

A Balliett & Fitzgerald Book
Design by Susan Canavan

Random House website address: www.randomhouse.com

Printed in the United States of America on acid-free paper

9 8 7 6 5 4 3 2

First Edition

Contents

Belly Basics:
The Conception

It began as a test order in early September 1994. Seventy kits for Bloomingdale's NYC. We took a deep breath and entered the store. It was only moments before we spotted it and smiled simultaneously. Everything had arrived in time for our Labor Day launch (how fortuitous). The white boxes with bold black lettering each read The Pregnancy Survival Kit® and were neatly stacked in rows of four. One on top of another, occupying two six-foot towers. We were playing in the big leagues now—and were plenty nervous. But as the friends and family who had come to wish us well were slowly elbowed out of the way by interested customers, we realized this was the birth of something big.

Our crazy new idea had worked. We were a success.

The idea itself was conceived one morning as we sat side by side in our matching work spaces on the eleventh floor of a Midtown office building in New York City. We were managing the marketing department at Henri Bendel, a women's retailer. Over our morning coffee, we hit on a topic we both felt passionate about: the complete lack of hip maternity clothes. Cherie had just returned from maternity leave, and we reminisced about the tying, wrapping, stretching, and pinning she regularly undertook in an effort to look good. With her belly back down to size, she was clearly happy to be back in her regular clothes. Jody, thinking of becoming pregnant herself and not looking forward to the offerings, wanted to delve deeper. As we analyzed the situation— what worked, what didn't—a lightbulb went on. A woman really needs only four key pieces as the core of her maternity wardrobe: a top, leggings, a skirt, and a dress that she can wear during the day and out at night. Pieces that look like the kind of clothes she'd wear if she weren't pregnant. Yes! The ideas began to fly. Then, at once, we stopped and stared at each other. Without realizing the massiveness of the project we were about to undertake, we simply said, "Let's do it!"

We instantly named it The Pregnancy Survival Kit for, to us, it was the only way to "survive" pregnancy in style. Ten months later, we had it in our hands. We scheduled a meeting with the divisional VP of Bloomingdale's (sneaking out from our "day" jobs). We hoped to get some constructive feedback—only in our dreams did we even consider that she'd place an order. What started out as a quiet meeting quickly turned into a frenzied scene. One buyer called in another and the whole place was buzzing. Anyone within earshot had to know what The Pregnancy Survival Kit was. After our meeting we rode down a crowded elevator and shot each other incredulous glances: "Did that just happen?" We had made our first sale—to none other than Bloomingdale's. When we hit the street we let out a big scream and realized a celebration was in order. The only problem was that it was late and Cherie was due home to relieve her baby-sitter while Jody had to run back to the office to finish some work. Taking a quick detour, we dashed into a store for a bottle of Moët, hopped onto a nearby concrete wall, and popped the cork. And with two Dixie cups we toasted to "Partners"!

Jody's Midtown apartment became our official headquarters. With a glass dining table as our desk, we went to work. We had two phones, a fax, and a prehistoric computer donated by Cherie's dad.

Bloomingdale's' test order sold out in three days and they quickly placed a reorder five times the size of the first. Belly Basics®, our new company, was up and running. Shortly thereafter, we appeared in our first publication, *New York* magazine, which was quickly followed by *Glamour*, the *Los Angeles Times*, *The New York Times*, and *Fortune*. We had become the company with the "it" kit.

Soon we were getting calls from buyers all over the world wanting to see our product. By Christmas 1994 we were selling the kit in the United Kingdom and Mexico and were poised to sign a licensing deal with Australia. And in New York, Bloomingdale's had become the first stop on every pregnant woman's shopping journey.

Today, Belly Basics is unique in the marketplace. We accommodate a pregnant woman's every desire, with style. Our minimal designs and distinctive packaging can be seen the world over. Spanning three continents, our Survival Kit fills the same needs in Osaka, Japan, as in Wichita, Kansas. Women just want to look good, period. And we are dedicated to making it happen.

Wonder of wonders . . .
You're Pregnant

We have each witnessed two miracles in our lives: the births of our children. If this sounds overly dramatic to you, just wait. From the moment your belly begins to grow until you hold your precious bundle in your hands, you will be continually startled by the sheer awesomeness of it. You'll see it start to unfold as your belly begins to round . . . when you hear the little heartbeat. It will continue to astound you when you feel the first kicks of life inside you. And as you watch your belly physically move with life inside. When the baby finally comes out, pushed by your own strength, you fully realize that, my god, you were carrying around a real live human being in your belly all this time. The enormity of the miracle hits you. And it doesn't end with the birth. In fact, it just begins. Each day the intensity of the miracle fills your head, as you watch your child flourish, change, and grow. Being a mom is a truly earth-shattering experience unlike anything you've experienced before.

You are pregnant. The journey begins

It happens immediately. You go from being yourself, familiar and comfortable, to instantly becoming someone completely different. All it takes is a plastic stick or a friendly doctor to say those two words you've been waiting to hear. And suddenly everything changes. When Jody was first pregnant she used to wake up every morning and turn to her husband, David, asking unbelievingly, "I'm pregnant?" She certainly didn't *feel* pregnant. She did feel strange, though. Very. Like she was finally a member of some grown-up club or something. You just feel different. But there's no sign of it anywhere. The queasiness, the expanding abdomen, the

big chest—these don't kick in until a little later. Initially, it's all mental. When Cherie took the home pregnancy test she waited the necessary three minutes and then made a nervous Daniel walk into the bathroom with her so they could witness the test result at exactly the same time. She wanted him to be a part of the excitement—and besides, she was too chicken to brave it alone. The test was positive. They stared at each other in disbelief. Cherie remembers this ticklish feeling inside of her and the funny little grin that slowly formed on Daniel's face as they stared at the pink square on the stick. They took a long, aimless walk down Third Avenue. Walking hand in hand, they needed time to think and digest a mixture of feelings. After several moments of silence they shared their thoughts. Turns out they were similar: happiness, excitement, and even slight trepidation at the unknown. Just sharing their feelings calmed them.

Once you've actually accepted it and allowed yourself to believe it, your mind starts racing with a million different issues. In many ways it's like getting engaged. Once you get over the initial rush of excitement, your mind drifts to: When will the wedding be? Whom will I ask to be my bridesmaids? What kind of dress will I wear? With a baby on the way, your mind begins to pulse in a similar way. What do you think the baby will look like? I hope she doesn't get my nose! Oh my god, where will he sleep? We've got to pick names. Wow, I've got to give up coffee and alcohol—today! Then your concerns might become slightly more concrete. How will we tell everyone? When do you think I'm going to start showing? I think I feel my body changing already. What in the world am I going to wear?

Here's where we come in. To be honest, getting dressed from here until delivery day does take some work. But it's something that, with just a little effort, anyone can do well. And that's the name of the game.

Pregnancy, our miracle of miracles, does completely change your body. It starts with your boobs. Tender and getting fuller by the hour, they are usually the first to take a hit.

Next you notice a general bloating. And then, as you progress into months two and three, you begin to feel yourself widening. Everywhere. Your hips, your butt, and your abs—yes, those stubborn little muscles that you've worked so hard to keep firm. They all expand to better carry your new occupant around. With every passing week you are going to get bigger, wider, and "fatter." That's what it's all about. No, we're not advocating total mayhem with your diet or exercise regime. What we're saying is that when you're pregnant, your body does what Nature has designed for it. Eating right and exercising will certainly make you feel and look better, but it won't change Nature's big plan. Don't try to fight it.

Once your body begins to change, it's probably time to announce the big news. This can be a bit nerve-racking. How will people respond? Will your friends be excited for you or might some of them be envious? How will you tell your parents if they don't already know? What will your boss say? These concerns are common. There's no way to know exactly how anyone will respond. When Jody announced her first pregnancy, she delivered her news slightly differently depending on whom she was telling. To her girlfriends—some single, some married, but none with children—she played it down during a "girls night out." To her surprise, they were so excited they didn't stop talking about it all evening. With her parents, she held nothing back. They knew almost as quickly as she and David did. Cherie, too, couldn't help but blurt it out to both their parents the very night she and Daniel found out. But Cherie held off telling her boss at the time until she was into her fifth month. Hesitant of rocking the boat, she waited until it was no longer an option, then she told him in an amusing way. She sat down in his office for her regular lunchtime chat. Instead of a sandwich, she pulled out a pint of chocolate Häagen-Dazs and a crunchy dill pickle. Waiting for him to notice what she was doing, she was poised and ready to dip the pickle in the ice cream. Thankfully, he looked up and saw the nasty combination. He understood immediately and they both started to laugh. Sharing the news with the "rest of the world" is exciting and wonderful (albeit a little stressful)—you are on center stage.

Your body is going to go through a metamorphosis. At times you will feel beautiful and special. At other times you will feel ugly and fat. Granted, it's difficult to sit back and watch as your body grows and grows . . . and grows, but if you keep it in perspective you'll be much happier. Your body is home to the baby for nine months. And believe us, they make themselves right at home. Even though it is your body, one that you have always tried to maintain, for the next nine months you've got a renter in there. He's in charge now, and there's no turning back. You might as well make the best of it. Try to play up your positive features to make you feel more like you. If you have good legs, show them off with a short dress or skirt. If your eyes are blue, play them up with the color shirt you choose. If you have sexy collarbones, make sure to show them off.

There will be times, nevertheless, when your emotions get the best of you and throw you completely off track. The good news is that this stage does pass quickly. But that little growing baby can wreak emotional havoc. At the beginning of Jody's pregnancy, everyone drove her crazy, including her husband. For some people, it's obsessive worrying that transpires. For others, it's complete grumpiness. Sometimes you'll want to be left alone, and at other times you'll crave companionship. Sometimes you can even become irrational. (Imagine that!)

When we were launching Belly Basics and Jody was in her sixth month, we had a brainstorming session with a packaging designer concerning our nearly perfected little white box. The meeting was nothing extraordinary. Neither were the designer's comments—they were quite good

Don't get carried away reading books on child rearing. While the baby is still growing in your womb, it's pretty hard to relate. You have no idea what kind of parenting style you're going to adhere to, nor what kind of child your little one will be. Save those books for when you really need them (and believe us, you will).

actually. But when Jody and Cherie got back to the office and summarized the meeting to decide what their next step would be, Jody flew off the handle. She was nearly hysterical (completely out of character) and insistent that we disregard the designer's suggestions. Nothing at all would change her mind. It wasn't until late that evening that she realized she had been on a hormonal roller-coaster ride and said to herself, What in god's name was I thinking? She quickly placed a late-night apology call to Cherie, who in turn laughed the whole thing off.

Your hormones most definitely are out of whack. There's no question about it. Of course, while it's happening to you, it doesn't feel like it's you who's acting strange. It really feels like it's everyone else—why is the whole world so annoying? When you're feeling your absolute worst, do try to remember that your husband or mate will feel your mood swings even more intensely than you (because more often than not, he's on the receiving end). He's there for you when you feel ugly and fat, when even strangers irk you, when you're a crying mess, and when you feel beautiful. Our advice? Be extra nice to him when you can tolerate the sight of him. He's yours for the long haul. Although you're the one carrying the baby, he is having a baby, too. He's going to be a dad. Show him that his next nine months aren't going to be a living hell filled with erratic mood swings, grouchiness, and complaining (though most of it will be). True, he'll be the one kicking back with a Rolling Rock while you fight off heartburn after a sip of Perrier, but keep in mind: You are privileged, honored if you will, to have a human life grow inside of you. And that's better than anything your husband will ever experience. Remember that.

Don't worry, be happy

There are so many things that we all obsess about during our pregnancies, especially during the first few months. Things like: Maybe I'm too old to have a baby. Are we tempting fate with number two or number three? And we've all had thoughts like: I don't feel pregnant right now. What if I'm not pregnant anymore? These are the kinds of things that will keep you tossing and turning at night. These are very real concerns that most women have. You have nine months to ponder and, trust us, you're going to ponder every conceivable situation. But we can assure you that these feelings of panic, which may be more acute at the beginning before you have the belly to prove that you are indeed pregnant, will most certainly lessen as your healthy baby continues to grow inside of you. As you begin to look more pregnant, and after you see a sonogram or two (those things are awesome), you'll begin to feel much more confident.

Once your belly becomes visible, you tend to become "public property." People somehow forget that there's actually a person underneath that big ole tummy. With strangers touching you at your every turn, it is hard to feel like it's the same old you in there. Even casual friends and coworkers will reach right out to caress your belly. We've all done it. This is why it's important to dress normally, the way you did before you became pregnant. You are going to be looked at now more than at any other time in your life. Try to stay away from bows and loud prints—the kind of clothes that shout an unnecessary "Hey look at me, I'm pregnant!" You will always get a bit of extra attention whether you're "asking" for it or not. If strangers do give your belly an unsolicited little pat, try to pay little mind. When Cherie was pregnant she interpreted it as an act of caring and kindness. And to Jody, it didn't feel like people were touching her belly, her skin—no, it felt more like they were touching her baby. It's nice to get the extra attention, even if just for a few minutes.

Pregnant women are an anomaly, a class unto themselves. And as your emotions and moods ride their course, making you and the people who love you completely bonkers, know that you are not alone. You are part of pack of women who consider grilled cheese at four in the morning to be quite normal, and the smell of salami to be a near-death experience. And each and every second of it is truly a miracle.

What Is Style?

"I'm three months pregnant and I'm feeling BIG. It's Monday morning, 8 A.M. I'm already late for work because I hit my snooze one too many times. I am standing at the door of my closet in my husband's wrinkled college T-shirt that I slept in the night before. . . . Help!"

We have certainly both been there, twice. You wake up tired and nauseous, and the last thing you want to do is think about whether you're in the mood for red or blue. There are enough important issues during your pregnant months to keep your mind occupied rather than letting it become consumed with what we have termed "the clothing dilemma." With just a little forethought and creativity, your nine months of pregnancy will be a fashion breeze.

Style. Ever present, always allusive, it's something most of us probably don't give much thought to on a regular basis. We simply get dressed each morning without serious consideration of an overriding fashion "theme" that propels us to dress a certain way. Now, as you embark on your nine-month journey of having to rethink your entire wardrobe, it becomes absolutely essential to spend some time considering personal style, whether yours is a style you were lucky enough to be born with, spent years developing, or, perhaps, don't even realize you have. The main point that we stress day in and day out is, at all costs, hold on to your style. Maintain it during your pregnancy. Your style before you became pregnant should continue to be your style during your pregnancy. You are still the same person. Why should your whole sense of style change just because the EPT stick turned pink? Along the same lines, why would you wear something when you're pregnant that you wouldn't normally wear? For years, women

looked at their nine-month pregnancies as a complete and total departure from their own personal style. Forced to wear the out-of-date offerings from maternity companies, women would buy and wear clothes that were simply just not them. Clothes with inferior fabrics, garish collars, silly oversized buttons, and grandmother-styling were all they had to choose from. (We all remember the *I Love Lucy* episodes with Lucy parading around in giant-sized polka dots and Peter Pan collars during her pregnancy with Little Ricky.)

It seemed crazy to us that pregnant women would sit back and accept this imposed, arbitrary style. We saw what was out there. And we definitely couldn't see ourselves wearing it. This is why we felt compelled to create something for pregnant women that was affordable, easy to wear, and basic. Clothing that allows you to freely express your own sense of style (we can't all have it as easy as a pregnant Madonna, who had the top runway designers at her beck and call whipping up a frock or two to accommodate her new figure).

It's probably taken you many years, possibly decades, to perfect your look. Experimenting with different trends and styles was what most of us did in high school, college, and even into our early twenties. Experimenting is crucial to building your own style. If you don't try something, you'll certainly never know if it works for you or not. Those lucky people with innate style who never seem to go through an experimental period are an exception. They were very obviously born with a knack to know just how to make clothes work for them. Jody's childhood friend Hilary, even back in junior high school in suburban Michigan, always seemed to look "put together." While others around her wore the latest seventies fads, colors, styles, etc., she seemed to remain "above it all" in her quietly cool clothes. We're sure that if we looked at pictures of what she actually wore then, the clothes would probably seem as goofy as the rest of our teenage clothes, but that's what style is all about. A person with natural-born style just exudes it. For the rest of us, it takes effort to know what works for us and what we like. We hope that at this stage in your life you are comfortable with your own style, even if you've never actually thought of it as your "style." But whatever you do, *don't abandon it now.* With all the crazy changes your body is going through and the entirely new dimensions your household will be facing, you need to feel like *you're still you.* Playing up your style during the next few months is crucial to maintaining your cohesive self.

Never get rid of anything in an animal print— it's a fashion perennial. It never goes out of style and always looks chic if it's worn sparingly and mixed with a solid black or white outfit. Whether it's on a scarf, a pair of leggings, a vest, a hat, or a belt, an animal print can work season after season, year after year.

While some people can instantly identify, even in one simple word, their own style, most of us can't. You might find it easier to think of people you know and then think about what *their* style is. This will help you define the main "arteries" of style in your own terms. From there, it will be easier to picture yourself as fitting into a broad category. Your style may cross over into a few different areas. Jody tends to dress classically on most days, but she loves to interject key trendy items here and there. Recently, on the airplane trip down to St. Bart's with David, she wore a classic black turtleneck, black cardigan sweater, and black driving moccasins. With those basics, she wore a pair of leopard print leggings. Her style is a mix. And we feel that makes for very interesting fashion.

Style? Who, me?!
The Main Arteries

Traditional. *Think Talbots and Brooks Brothers.*

Classic. *Picture Grace Kelly, Audrey Hepburn, and Catherine Deneuve.*

Classic with a twist. *Perhaps Uma Thurman or Julia Roberts in a Chanel jacket and faded blue jeans.*

Artistic/creative. *We all know someone who fits this description—usually ethnic prints, beaded necklaces, "hand-knit" sweaters, and other artful pieces.*

Trendy. *Always in the latest fads—picture the entire casts of 90210 and Melrose Place.*

Downtown hip. *Drew Barrymore, Pamela Anderson, or other leather-clad babes.*

Easygoing basics. *Lauren Hutton or Martha Stewart—picture sweaters and jeans, simple jewelry, comfortable shoes.*

Accessory-based. *The focus is on earrings, bracelets, necklaces. New items purchased each season tend to be jewelry, belts, shoes—Ivana Trump could be considered the quintessential accessory-based woman.*

While the list could go on forever, these categories seem to be the broadest, most obvious ones. Once you have honed in on the areas that best fit the way you like to see yourself, you'll be better able to visualize what your style is. But of course, style is not quite that simple. Your personality plays a huge role in what motivates you to get dressed each day. From the main arteries of style flow the veins that really stamp your individuality and make your style your own. Our friend Valerie, an accessories merchandiser, is always classically dressed. Her personality, delightfully refined and somewhat reserved, is reflected in how she adapts her classic style. For her, there is no straying from classics. Crisply attired in beautifully tailored clothing, she always wears a richly colored silk scarf and a pair of delicate, color-coordinated ballet-slipper flats. Her jewelry is simple and bold: a shiny wood cuff or a necklace with large discs of brushed metal. You'll never catch her strolling the streets of Manhattan without her button earrings and a fabulous link bracelet! Think about your own personality. Whether you've considered it before or not, you should know that your personality *is* at the root of your style, constantly propelling you to dress a certain way.

Give some thought to your personality. Do you tend to be:

Conservative?   Serious?
Cool and Collected? *Humorous?*
Colorful? *Quiet?* **No-nonsense?**
Daring? *Romantic?*
Modern? Unpredictable?
The life of the party?

Cherie, for example, wears a lot of simple clothes to work. Her wardrobe includes lots of solid clothes with straight lines in basic colors. She stays clear of patterns and too many brights. Her accessories tend to be small and simple, like the narrow platinum band she wears on her left hand or the simple diamond studs she wears in her ears. Her look is minimal. But on the weekends when she's at home with her husband and kids, she's relaxed and has a little more fun with her clothes. She often interjects color and even some prints—a nice respite from the neutrals of her workweek. This better reflects her weekend mood. Your mood and purpose will often help determine a particular day's style. Sometimes the type of day you have planned or even the people you are scheduled to meet may influence the clothing choices that you make in the morning. We both make it a practice to check our appointment books before we get dressed each day.

We went to college with a girl named Nancy. (Coincidentally, we *both* went to the University of Michigan—our meeting up years later was pure fate!) She wore gym shoes every single day—gym shoes with leggings, gym shoes with jeans, gym shoes with pants. She wore a lot of sweatshirts and button-down shirts. If you were to ask her what her style was, she would probably have said, "Style? I have no style!" But to the contrary, she had a very definite style. It mirrored her personality—warm, affable, and comfortable. And that was her style: comfortable clothes, easy-going basics. And if she were to start wearing pumps and earrings, she just wouldn't be Nancy.

Personal style helps define who a person is. A few months ago we found ourselves in the middle of a search for a new public relations firm for Belly Basics. It just so happened that we set up two meetings Monday morning, back to back. At 10:00 a woman named Elaine arrived wearing all black. She wore a beautifully tailored pant suit with a silk georgette scarf and delicate earrings, and her hair was sleekly pulled back into a knot. Her coat was simple black wool, but had a certain flair as it fell around her. It was clear that she had a great sense of style. It was unimportant whether the clothes were "designer" or not; what *was* important was that in just a few minutes of meet and greet, we felt a beaming

confidence from this woman. We figured her to be organized, efficient, and "with it." One hour later our next appointment was ushered in. Her name was Janice. She, too, was wearing black (we *are* in New York, after all), but her sweater was oversized, boxy, and less professional, her pants were creased, and her shoes had been through one too many Manhattan rainstorms. To us, her slightly disheveled style spoke volumes about her personality: a little disorganized and perhaps less serious about her work. A person's style often sets a mood. We're not saying that you need to dress like Elaine; what we are saying is that knowing your own style makes it easier to understand how you appear to others.

Now that you've gotten a better handle on exactly what we mean when we talk about style, let's move on to how we're going to keep it in place during the next nine months. Starting with your own closet, we'll help you sort through what you already have that, believe it or not, may still work.

Let's start at the very beginning . . .

Closet Shopping

The first thing you need to do is assess your everyday clothing needs. Do you go to work each day? Do you stay at home? Maybe you work part-time. What do your weekends consist of? Entertaining? Going out to "hot spots"? Play groups with your older child? Obviously, all of these activities will require different types of clothing. Don't panic. You probably have many things in your closet (much more than you may think) that will get you most, if not all, of the way through. Clothing that you already own and feel comfortable in should be the mainstay of your nine-month wardrobe. We believe pregnancy should be a wonderful continuation of your life, not a compromise of your style. Why should you dress differently just because you're pregnant? Our philosphy is that in order for a pregnant woman to wear the clothes she's most comfortable in, she needs certain "underpinnings"—the basics that will adapt to her swiftly growing belly and yet, at the same time, will allow her to wear her favorite sweater or blazer. When we launched The Pregnancy Survival Kit in 1994, our four essential pieces—a tunic top, leggings, a short slim skirt, and an A-line dress—were offered in black only. Black, when worn from head to toe, acts as a canvas. You build on it, adding your personal imprint: clothing and accessories from your own closet.

The good news is that you don't have to go out and buy a thousand dollars' worth of maternity duds. You can still count on wearing your favorite blazer or the striped button-down shirt you bought from the J. Crew catalog a year ago and have worn like a uniform ever since. Dresses, vests, and even many of your pants can all still work. When Jody was pregnant with her second baby, she wore a charcoal gray single-breasted blazer all the time during the first seven months of her pregnancy, slowly leaving more and more of the buttons undone with each passing week. By adding a loose-fitting shirt

Take as many snapshots as you can of your growing belly. If you're not into showing a whole lot of skin, do as Cherie did when she was pregnant: Wear a black unitard for the picture. It's just as effective and it's actually more graphic. Black-and-white film will also help make for a nice photo composition later. You might balk about posing in front of a camera now, but these snapshots will be an invaluable memento after the baby is born.

under the blazer, she was able to continue to wear it by pairing it with Belly Basics leggings. Cherie's favorite from her own wardrobe was a long knit cardigan that worked over a straight ankle-length skirt. Barring any extraordinarily excessive weight gain, you'll be able to wear your "outer" pieces most of the way, if not all of the way, through your pregnancy. As long as you have a few core maternity pieces to properly fit your belly, your favorite clothes will look right—and feel right—as your tummy grows. You might wear them in ways that you never would have before. That's great! Be creative. Accessories are the key to helping you extend the life of the clothes you already own (and to stretching the few maternity clothes you do have to buy). Scarves, jewelry, and shoes will all become indispensable fashion tools to you now (we delve further into exactly how in the upcoming chapters).

Taking inventory

With this "keeping your style" philosophy in mind, take inventory of what you already own. Set aside an hour of your time and do a thorough once-over in your closet. You'll need to keep an open mind. Let's face it, your needs have changed and will continue to change for the next nine months. You just might need to tuck your favorite jeans away—maybe you'll be able to wear them for several more months, but trust us, you *will* reach a point where you will need stow them. We suggest you keep them on the top shelf (it's just for a few months—we know, it hurts) because experience has shown us that if the clothes that no longer fit you aren't staring you in the face each time you open your closet, you'll have an easier time adapting to your new, temporary way of dressing. Think of it as a "forbidden fruit" and don't tempt yourself. We suggest you rearrange your closet so that the things you can continue to wear are front and center, while the things you definitely can't (or shouldn't) are pushed out of sight.

As you go through your closet and drawers, article by article, think about the different activities that make up your day—weekdays and weekends. This is a broad exercise to get you thinking about what types of clothes you already own that can work while you're pregnant. In the next several chapters, we'll analyze exactly how and when to wear these pieces.

When you begin your "closet shopping,"

think in terms of categories. The main point is to discern what's workable from each. Once you've done that, you'll have a much clearer picture of where your pregnancy wardrobe stands.

Let's start at the bottom, with the bare necessities:

Underwear

Understandably, comfortable underwear becomes very important to you when your entire middle begins to resemble a beach ball. Uncomfortable underwear can make a person pretty cranky and, for this reason, many women become passionate about what type of underwear they choose to wear. We both fell into this category because comfort was the number-one consideration for both of us during our pregnant months. Jody wore her thong undies throughout. Under nonpregnant conditions, she found they were the most comfortable style, so why would she wear anything else during her pregnancy? As her belly grew, she simply increased the size of the underwear. Cherie, conversely, chose to wear maternity

underclothes that, for her, were ultracomfortable. Her main objective was that they be unobtrusive. They were really simple—soft cotton (the kind that improves with each washing) with a loose men's-style elastic band that rested below her tummy. They were bikinis, but a far cry from the imported silk bikinis she had treated herself to on her last birthday. Whichever you prefer, make sure they fit. Improperly fitting underwear can be a real mood inhibitor. If you're in comfortable panties, you've got it made. And if you're like our friend Melissa in Chicago, you may want to abandon underwear altogether during your pregnancy. Talk about comfort!

Getting back to your closet, we say, "Out with the old and in with the new" when it comes to underwear. Give your favorite blue silk bikinis a rest. As your belly gets bigger, your underwear gets smaller. You'll end up stretching out and ruining all your best underpants. Go out and buy the cheapest panties you can find and make sure they are all cotton. If ever you needed breathable panties, it's now.

You have two options in terms of the types of underwear to buy—maternity and nonmaternity. Both will work so it's a matter of personal preference. If you ask fifty mothers what they wore during their pregnancies (which, incidentally, we did), you'll get about fifty different answers. If you choose regular panties (nonmaternity) just buy them one or two sizes bigger. Buy them at any discount or department store where you think you'll find the best selection and the best price. The other option is to go to a maternity store. You can pick a pair like

Tips to remember when you're undie shopping

- If you're planning on buying regular panties (nonmaternity), remember to go up at least one size, probably two.
- Even with maternity underwear, buy bigger than you currently need so you don't have to come back again in a few months.
- Don't compromise your style. If you wore bikinis before you were pregnant, buy bikinis. Thongs, too.
- Buy 100 percent cotton panties. They have the most breathability. Remember, the name of the game is comfort. Silk panties are comfortable but are more costly and not quite as breathable.
- The waistband should not be too tight. If it has elastic at all, make sure it's either covered (so that it is a bit smoother and lies more comfortably on your skin) or loose fitting.
- They should be sexy. Don't think you have to go the old-maid route just because you're pregnant (unless of course, that was your style before you got pregnant!). You want to feel good when you put them on in the morning. Your husband might also enjoy looking at them when he checks out your growing belly.

Cherie wore—with a waistband that goes under the belly (the package will say bikini). Or there is another style of maternity underwear that actually covers your entire belly. Our feeling is that the latter might tend to make you feel even more unlike yourself than you do already. Who walks around with their underwear pulled up to their boobs?

Cherie's college friend Diane lives in Washington, D.C. On a business trip to promote Belly Basics, Cherie stopped by for a visit. She hadn't seen her during her entire pregnancy and now Diane's new baby was seven months old. Cherie, Diane, and her husband, Matt, were sitting in Diane and Matt's living room. While Diane was giving the baby a bottle, Matt said, "Would you like to see the most beautiful woman in the world?" Without waiting for a response, he whipped out a leather-bound album titled "The Belly"—and it was an album of just that. Each page was a close-up shot of Diane's belly (starting out small, then growing as the pages—and weeks—progressed). Matt had taken a picture

of Diane at the end of each of her forty weeks. Every page was a photo of her belly, and in each picture she was wearing a pretty, sexy pair of underwear—in different colors, sometimes in silk, sometimes in cotton, and usually with a touch of lace. Matt was happy to see that Cherie was impressed by his touching "belly" book. But really Cherie was utterly amazed that her very conservative buddy was sporting such sexy undies, pregnant and all.

Bras

We know, the last time you read about bras you were probably thirteen and about to buy your first one. They're not the most riveting of subjects, and a discussion of them in a book would not normally be necessary. But as we've said, your needs have certainly changed . . . or are in the process of changing dramatically, and one of the first places you'll feel physical change is in your chest. Your breasts seem to change immediately. All of a sudden you look down and you've got these big, round pendulous boobs. Yeah, *you're pregnant all right!* A properly fitting bra is a major necessity every step of the way. Chest size in nonpregnant women varies considerably. Chest size in pregnant women varies radically. Honestly, some women's chests get so big that you can't even imagine the alphabet letters go that high! Your chest *will* change, probably more than once. You definitely have to be prepared to meet those changes. Bras are something that, unless you are one of a very tiny percentage of exceptionally small-breasted women, you will need to buy.

We found in talking to hundreds of women—pregnant or not—that bra styles are a very personal choice. Women develop a preference before they're pregnant and rarely change their preference after they're pregnant. If you have an allegiance to underwires, you're going to like them when you're pregnant, too. If you can't stand the feel of wires, they're going to bug you even more during your nine months. A bra is the one thing it seems all women buy in their first trimester. We seem to find more pregnant women in the lingerie department than anywhere else in the store. It's definitely a pregnant woman's first stop.

You may find yourself thinking as you get bigger that wearing a bra to sleep would be a good idea. You may not do this under normal circumstances, but your pregnant months are definitely *not* normal. For women whose breasts get big and tender, it becomes quite uncomfortable to sleep without a bra. If you're feeling uncomfortable, try sleeping in a light, unstructured bra, possibly in a cotton/Lycra blend, which will give you some support as you toss and turn, trying to find a suitable position in bed. (If you have an old bodysuit that you were able to wear without a bra, take scissors and cut off the snaps (including the extra fabric that would normally cover your whole belly). Just make sure you don't cut off too much. Try it on first and make a mark on the bodysuit where you want the customized "bra" to end. This makes a great, comfortable, and inexpensive sleep bra (it's also perfect to wear around the house, which Jody did all the time). Cherie preferred to sleep in a bra-styled workout tank. These too are very comfortable and supportive without having wires or straps. They are made out of a

Our rules of thumb when buying a new bra

• Ask for help! Get professionally measured. We know it's awkward having someone measure your chest, but if you purchase the right sized bra from the beginning, you'll be much happier throughout your nine months. Women who work in lingerie departments or lingerie stores are experts in the field of "fit," and they are very used to helping pregnant women. Don't feel funny telling her your secret (even if your own friends don't know you're pregnant). You can whisper if you have to. Knowing that you're pregnant will probably change the type of bra she would suggest and will increase your comfort level with the whole process. And besides, it might actually be a relief for you to let the cat out of the bag.

• After you select a style that you think will work, buy just one to try. Before buying it in a whole color assortment, make sure you love the way it wears. If the store delivers, be sure to take the phone number when you leave so you don't have to physically return to the store. If you are happy with the bra, call from home and place an order.

• Once you've made your choice, buy in quantity—at least three or four. Don't skimp and think that you can make do with some of your old bras. You want to be comfortable, and you also want to look comfortable. A properly sized bra will do that.

• Now is not the time to be experimenting with new styles. Don't change the style of your bra just because you're pregnant. If you like one hook in the back, stick to one hook; if you like a bra to push you up, go for it.

Don't let anyone tell you that pregnant women don't wear *that* kind of bra. We've said it before and we'll say it again: Don't compromise your style. Cherie went to Victoria's Secret and bought three new bras in the exact style she wore before she was pregnant but in a bigger cup size. There was no way she was going to try on a million different styles when she knew there was a tried-and-true style that already worked for her.

• If you started with a big chest before you became pregnant, your chest may now be absolutely huge. If your chest is growing exponentially faster than your belly and doesn't appear to be stopping, you should go to a maternity store for a bra. They typically stock large-size bras.

heavier cotton/Lycra fabric that really holds your chest in place. Believe us when we say your chest ain't going nowhere in one of those!

Hosiery

You'll be able to get by with your existing hosiery until it gets uncomfortable—somewhere in your second trimester. Sounds basic, but that's pretty much the rule. If you don't have the need for hosiery very often and only wear it on special occasions, try folding it down underneath your belly. This works before your belly gets *grande*—at that point, you'll need to switch to maternity pantyhose. No matter how comfortable your underwear, you'll never be fully at peace until your hosiery feels good!

Jewelry

Whether jewelry is a part of your everyday style or not, it's a godsend when you're pregnant. If you've never cared for jewelry, or just never bothered with it, then this is the time to explore. The reasons are myriad. As you'll soon see, the bigger the belly, the less options for different clothing. Consequently, the easiest way to change your look and keep you from boredom is through jewelry. Check your jewelry boxes for these (or borrow from your mom, sister, or friends):

Necklaces. Look for long strands, choker-length, or anything in between. Pearls, beads, pendants, etc., are all going to be great assets to you. A beaded necklace or pendant can help divert attention away from the "bull's-eye" point of your belly. It also may lend a totally different feeling to a simple black dress, tunic, or blouse.

Bracelets. In many ways these are even easier to wear than necklaces. Look for gold, silver, or beaded. They might not make a huge statement outwardly, but you'll feel different wearing them, giving new life to the same key maternity clothes. And a cuff bracelet in gold, tortoise, silver, etc., is a fashion statement by itself. Jody wore her bold silver cuff frequently with her black cotton/Lycra dress. Delicate bangles are great, too. Cherie has four thin silver bands that can be worn either together or

separately. She picked them up in Mexico years ago when she was single (on one of those trips where all you do is lie out in the sun, drink margaritas, and shop the flea markets). She hadn't worn these bracelets in years and one day when she was pregnant they resurfaced and she slipped them on. Simply shaped, they were the perfect accent for her solid tunics.

Pins. Yes, pins! If you work, a pin is great to stick on your jacket lapel or right onto your shirt or tunic top. You can even leave it on your jacket while it hangs in the closet. In the morning when you toss it on, you'll be happy it's there waiting for you. After Jody's first baby was born, her friend Jane gave her a little pin that was a miniature baby in brushed gold. During her second pregnancy, it became a fixture for her on tunics and blazers. It was a conversation piece and a great way to get people to notice something *other than her belly*. Dig up any that you have.

Earrings. Earring styles vacillate from big and bold to tiny, *tiny* and barely noticeable. No matter which are currently en vogue, earrings can totally change the statement you make with your clothing. If you are not a necklace or a bracelet person, perhaps you have an easier time wearing earrings (our friend Susie virtually sleeps in her earrings—silver hearts, gold balls, or silver knots—and she never ever wears any other jewelry). If you don't have pierced ears, try a pair of clip-ons. Today's clip-ons look nothing like the kind your grandmother wore. Just making an effort to wear different earrings (assorted shapes, metals, stones, etc.) is an easy way to lend a new slant to your outfit.

Handbags

For everyday schlepping, it is mandatory to make sure that the bag you're toting around is comfortable on your shoulder, your arm, and your back. If you're anything like we are, your bag is probably stuffed to the brim with everything from the everyday basics (wallet, makeup, sunglasses) to a book (maybe even this one!), a cellular phone, a snack (a *must* while pregnant), and even a bottle of H_2O. Those things are heavy. The weight of your bag can really throw off your posture if you're not careful. Even though your bag might look great, don't sacrifice comfort for style. Choose something else that's a little easier on your body. If you don't find anything that's comfortable, think about picking up an inexpensive backpack for the duration of your pregnancy. They come in all shapes and sizes, colors, and fabrics. Just slip it on your back and the weight is equally distributed. Another great thing about a backpack is that you'll use it after your baby is born. Even if you buy a classic diaper bag for the first year or so, you'll find that, as your child gets older, a backpack becomes a better and more versatile option. Also look for interesting colors, patterns, or fabrics when choosing your bag. This will help give your outfit a little oomph.

Scarves

We could write an entire book on the merits of scarves. Quite simply, there is nothing better—or easier—to give your look versatility. A beautifully tied scarf brings a completely new dimension to your wardrobe.

How to wear a scarf

The first thing to keep in mind with a scarf is that its basic shape will dictate how it's worn. Some of the most basic shapes and easiest ways to wear scarves include:

A big square scarf
• Fold it into one big triangle, drape it over your shoulders, and tie it with a simple knot. This works well if you want to show the pattern on the scarf. It's great for work because it's very professional and businesslike.

• Try folding it so that it becomes long and about two to three inches wide. Wrap it around your neck and tie it loosely or wrap it around twice and knot it. This type of fold does not show as much of the pattern.

Oblong
• Toss it over your shoulder. This is great for evening. It looks romantic and feminine.
• Wrap it a few times around your neck and finish it with a knot.

Pocket square
• Fold it long and straight, then loosely tie around the neck. This is a

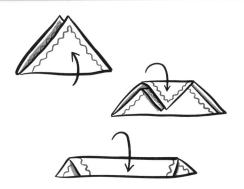

great way to add color around your face without making much of a scarf "commitment."

• Stick it in the breast pocket of a blazer. This is its true intention and it can look very smart placed there.

Scarves can help you "stretch" the styling options of the clothes you already own, as well as give your maternity staples a whole new look. Revisit scarves you already own (even the discards—like the floral one your Aunt Roberta gave you for Christmas that you vowed you'd never wear). With a bigger you, a scarf may take on a whole new look. Throughout most of the chapters in this book, we've given different styling options for tying scarves. You should definitely pull yours out from wherever they may be stashed, and keep them in a place where you'll be constantly reminded of them. Scarves are great to borrow from your mom (or even your mother-in-law); all moms have a stash of scarves tucked away somewhere. The more exotic the better. Try any and all fabrics, from velvet to cotton to silk moirée. During a recent TV segment we were doing in Nashville, we demonstrated how a scarf can change an entire look. The first model came out in black Belly Basics from head to toe. Just before the second model made her entrance (also in all black), we quickly wrapped a scarf around her neck. *Voilà!* The studio audience immediately broke into *ooohs* and *aaahs* of admiration at how this simple scarf gave the outfit color and something even more important: attitude.

Shoes

We'll start with a little antecdote. Last summer when Jody was seven months pregnant with her second baby, the thermometer suddenly skyrocketed around the first week in June. By the end of the day, her feet, which had been fairing quite well inside their regular shoes, quickly swelled up like balloons. She limped all the way to Penn Station, feeling like someone had secretly taken her size-8 loafers and replaced them with a size 6½. She missed her train by mere seconds because she couldn't make her usual mad dash to NJ Transit. People were actually stopping her and asking if she was okay—as if there was really something wrong. That entire week, with the temperature hovering around ninety, she found nothing that worked. In a panic she called her old roommate Flo, a shoe buyer at a major department store who had suffered through the previous summer's heat with her own pregnant belly. Needless to say, Flo came up with the best shoe ever. Jody immediately had them sent to her overnight, sight unseen. She was pleasantly surprised when they arrived. They were somewhat sporty black patent-leather ballet flats with a thick rubber bottom. They supported her foot because the sole was about an inch thick, and they had a tiny heel, perhaps a half inch or so. She bought them a full size larger than normal to allow room for swelling (something you should probably do whether it's hot or cold outside). This, plus the fact that they were incredibly comfortable shoes, helped get her through a killer summer. They worked with little dresses and with leggings and were for her the perfect summer pregnancy shoe.

Don't panic and think you're going to have to rush out and buy *this* shoe. You probably already have shoes in your wardrobe that will work beautifully. What you need to keep in mind is that your foot is going to "grow," literally. Some women's feet simply swell, eventually returning to normal size. Other women have feet that actually grow one shoe size during pregnancy, and never go back! But don't assume that, just because your shoes are feeling tight, you've outgrown them for good. It may just be temporary. Either way, you've got to find at least one versatile pair of shoes that you can live in during pregnancy. Make sure they are somewhat structured and support your feet. If not, they can actually be detrimental. Think of all that extra weight you're carrying around—it's got to be supported somewhere. Make sure the sole is fairly thick (*no*, you can't wear your gym shoes every day.) Because black is the most versatile color, we recommend that your everyday shoes be black. You may end up living in a shoe that you barely had use for before your pregnancy. For work and for formal occasions, stay away from high heels if possible; they are painful when you're pregnant, no two ways about it. And painful feet will make for a miserable day (sort of like uncomfortable undies). For times when you need to be dressier, wear stacked low

heels. If you need to buy a new pair, definitely buy them a half size bigger than normal. You won't regret it.

Button-down shirts/blouses

There are two types of button-down collared shirts that we need to think about—fitted and loose. You may have already shoved the fitted shirts up on a top shelf somewhere (maybe behind your jeans) because you're so sure you won't be able to wear them. Wrong. Get 'em back down. We love the look of a crisp shirt collar peeking out from underneath a tunic top (maternity sized) or a sweater—at least for the first half of your pregnancy, while it's still comfortable. Just unfasten the bottom buttons as your belly grows. No one but you will know.

A loose-fitting blouse is great unbuttoned over a T-shirt or a tunic for a totally different look. Look for shirts that are longer in length that will work as a layering piece and will also cover your bottom and thighs. A shirt like this will work throughout most of your pregnancy. Don't forget to raid your husband's closet for his button-downs—denim, flannel, and oxford cloth shirts—they all work. Lisa, Cherie's hair stylist, loved wearing her husband's shirt during the day when she was pregnant, especially at work. She enjoyed the faint smell of his cologne and the feel of his soft shirt next to her skin. With *their* baby in her belly, it was comforting to feel his presence during her hectic day.

Sweaters

As you stand in front of your closet to begin your morning ritual of choosing the day's outfit, you can't help but look longingly at some of your old favorites. Maybe it's the ice blue sweater with the baby cable stitch that somehow managed to make your cheeks look rosy even when you weren't wearing any makeup. Or maybe it's the charcoal gray shetland you've had since college, the one that you religiously wore during finals week because it brought you good luck. Although

An extra sweater is a great "tool" to have at your side for crazy, hormone-induced temperature swings. It's quite normal to go from uncomfortably hot to absolutely freezing in a mere matter of minutes.

these sweaters suddenly look more like doll clothes than things that would ever fit over the new curvaceous shape you're sporting, there is still a small glimmer of hope that you may be able to continue wearing them. It just takes a bit more creativity than before. You can tie one around your shoulders. For example, this looks good on top of a cotton button-down shirt or a simple blazer. It adds a pop of color next to your face while adding another element to your day's outfit.

You can also wrap a sweater around your waist (that is, while you still have something resembling a waist). Sometimes you can actually extend the life of a particular pair of pants by covering the waistband with the wrapped sweater.

The one type of sweater that you'll actually be able to wear throughout—and you can really *wear* these—is a tunic (defined as having a wide bottom rather than a tightly ribbed bottom). These are great with leggings, pants, and skirts. As your belly grows, the tunic will continue to fit your expanding belly. Some women end up spending most of their pregnancies in tunic sweaters with leggings (not the most creative look, but it's certainly up there in terms of comfort). Be wary of 100 percent cotton sweaters—they can easily stretch out, completely losing their shape. (A quick wash can sometimes correct this if you're lucky.) Sweaters to put away on a high shelf somewhere? Cropped, body-hugging, or favorite tight sweaters that you don't want to risk stretching out (maybe you have a seventeen-year-old sister who can use these).

Do you have any cardigans? We hope so, because cardigans are probably one of the most versatile items of clothing for a pregnant woman. Wool or cashmere is the most useful anytime of the year, but lightweight cotton can also be worn year-round. Wear it closed or open during the beginning months until it starts getting tight and then definitely leave it open over a loose oxford shirt, cotton crewneck sweater, or basic T-shirt. It's a great substitute for a blazer.

Furthermore, cardigans are key for nursing moms because you can unbutton just a few buttons at a time, keeping the exposed skin to a minimum.

A cardigan is one of a few items we would tell you to go out and buy if you don't already have one (maybe at the Limited or at a discounter like Loehmann's).
- Look for "open" bottoms that hang straight down.
- Make sure it's a deep solid color, preferably black, navy, or charcoal. These tones are much more slimming than brighter colors and will likely coordinate with more in your wardrobe.
- You shouldn't label this in your mind as a pregnancy purchase either. It's certainly something you'll wear post-belly.

T-shirts

Some people wear T-shirts day in and day out, regardless of season. If you're one of them you'll already have a whole arsenal of basic white T-shirts that will work with you as your belly grows. The only thing that changes is the way you'll wear them. Depending on the size you normally wear, a T-shirt will fit most of the way through your pregnancy as a perfect "underneath" layer for tunics, jackets, shirts, and vests. It will stretch easily across the belly, too. When your own T-shirts completely stop fitting, just pick up a couple of packs of XL 100 percent cotton men's T-shirts. Try Hanes, Fruit of the Loom, or a department store's private label brand—go to Kmart or a local department store—to get you through the rest of your pregnancy. Give them to your husband when you're done. Even if you

Why T-shirts? Here are five good reasons:
1. It's the perfect layering piece. It keeps you warm—Jody never went outside during her winter pregnancy without one underneath her tunic or even her dress.
2. You can get by without buying a larger size than the one you already own (especially if it's going to be worn under a tunic).
3. A T-shirt in a color other than white—say blush, yellow, or sky blue—when worn under a cardigan or solid shirt, can add a nice pop of color to your outfit.
4. It looks clean and crisp, and, when worn with a feminine touch, like a strand of choker pearls, it looks soft and sophisticated.
5. It's the world's most comfortable nightgown. Oversized tees are our all-time favorite to wear to sleep. It seems like such a waste to spend money on pajamas or nightshirts when you have a soft T-shirt sitting right in your dresser drawer (or your husband's). You probably own a few that have been washed oh, say, two hundred times, and are much softer than a new cotton nightgown that would come out of the store too starched and crisp.

aren't normally a T-shirt person, we do suggest buying a pack or two. Both Cherie and Jody continued to wear their own smaller T-shirts throughout their pregnancies. We both liked the smooth lines better underneath our clothes. Granted, our favorite old-time tees barely made it over the belly, but since it was merely a layering piece it didn't really matter (except at times when your outer shirt inadvertently lifts up and you feel like one of those fat truck drivers with a bulging beer belly).

Blazers

Don't rule them out so fast. This is one category in particular in which it really pays off to find some of your pre-pregnancy duds that'll work. A blazer always helps you look pulled together, whether for work or for going out to dinner. It will continue to be an essential part of your wardrobe during your pregnancy, just as it was before. Take each one out of your closet and try it on. Don't just look at your favorite blazers. Check out the ones that have been pushed aside or even moved to another closet because they aren't your everyday picks. In your current condition, they might quickly become staples. We beg you to give your own blazers a try because most of the ones you'll find in the maternity shops are bad news. They tend to be expensive, made of inferior fabrics, and designed with styling that is usually all wrong. Now is not the time in your life to compromise your style, standards, and taste level—or to drop a bundle of money at a maternity store. Our feeling is, if the blazer fits, wear it. And many of your blazers will, in fact, still fit.

We find that pregnant women don't necessarily layer enough because they think all of the layers must be maternity clothes. They also tend to think that layering makes them appear bigger. Neither of these is true. You can layer nonmaternity with maternity. And when done properly, layering can even be slimming (we'll go more into detail on exactly how in upcoming chapters).

What fits best? A jacket that's a bit longer and hits your leg in the middle portion of your thigh. Fingertip length is a good measure. A longer-length blazer looks great because it balances the weight of your rapidly growing belly. The cut of the blazer should be full, not close to your body. Blazers with tie fronts, selfbelts, and cut-away styling will work particularly well. You're in luck if you own one because you should be able to get away with it throughout most if not all of your pregnancy.

Single-breasted versus double-breasted? No question, single-breasted blazers are easier to work with. Assuming they fit the above criteria, they almost always look great. Double-breasted are a little trickier but are

tie-front blazer

fitted blazer

still totally workable—just don't expect to close them. At the beginning of your pregnancy, double-breasted blazers look great worn open over skirts, leggings, or pants (this happens to have been Jody's favorite look). When your belly really gets enormous though, double-breasted blazers become unwearable—they look silly over a huge, bulging belly. If you put on a double-breasted jacket, and you look in the mirror and something just doesn't look right, accept it and try a different look.

Fitted blazers can be worn only at the very beginning of your pregnancy when you can wear them by buttoning just the top two or three buttons. After that, move them to the back of the closet. Cropped or bolero

double-breasted blazer

jackets should immediately be put in the back of your closet—nothing looks worse than a short jacket on a pregnant body.

Dark colors work best (this doesn't mean black only: colors like navy, charcoal, and tweed are all great) and try to keep details to a minimum. Avoid exaggerated shapes, like a dolman sleeve, which adds extra inches. Shaped or square shoulders will help balance out the proportions of your bulging torso. But beware—shoulder pads that are too big can make you look big all over.

Clearly, not all women can wear a nonmaternity blazer or jacket through the duration of their pregnancy. It does depend on how your body decides to carry the baby and how much weight you gain. As we all know very well, pregnant women come in all shapes and sizes. A jacket might not fall correctly on a woman who is carrying very wide around her hips. As a matter of fact, it could look quite absurd—like she was wearing someone else's jacket. Cherie has a friend, Lori, who

happened to carry mostly in her hips and butt. The best looks on her were all-around loose-fitting garments. Her blazers were too constricting and didn't fit her from day one, so Lori substituted a lot of soft cardigan-styled jackets in their place. They were loose and hit her about an inch below her bum. She wore a cardigan-style jacket in the same way we suggest wearing your blazer—as a layering piece to pull together an entire look.

Whatever you do, don't resort to wearing your husband's blazer. This is one category for which raiding his closet is a resounding no-no. A man's jacket is tailored for a man's hulking

37
closet
shopping

Keep in mind that when you want to wear a blazer with a pair leggings (which, if you take our advice, will probably be often), your blazer will need to be long and full enough to cover your bottom and your thighs, not to mention the tunic or shirt you wear under it.

body. Even if the two of you are similiar in stature, the shoulders are way too padded for a woman, and the proportions are all wrong.

The only way you might, and we say *might*, be able to pull this off is if the blazer is extremely loose and unstructured and you wear it sort of like a jacket instead of as part of your outfit. The key? The shoulders must be soft and pliable. If they stick out from your body like a linebacker's, you'll look foolish. Trust us.

Ribbed turtlenecks and other knit shirts

Don't discount any of these shirts during your pregnancy—they should not be cast aside with your tightest jeans. Like the T-shirt, they make great layering pieces. Each should be looked at separately. It's really a matter of how you like to dress and how you'll be comfortable dressing as your belly gets bigger. Jody wore her tight ribbed turtlenecks and other long-sleeved shirts for several months under her cardigans and blazers. But like blazers, there are a few styles that you'll truly be hard-pressed to wear. Do put away bodysuits (unless you're willing to cut off the snaps), cropped tops, cut-off shirts, halters, and tube tops.

Pants

Most women immediately think that they have to stop wearing all of their pants, but that is not so. Some pants will work nearly all of the way through; others will work for a short time with a few buttons left open, zippers unzipped, and maybe even a safety pin here or there. The pants currently in your closet will get you farther than you think.

Fitted trousers. Fitted pants are very workable until you really begin to show—at which point you'll find yourself bulging out of them. The truth of the matter is that you, and only you, know when your pants are starting to feel too snug and don't fit well anymore. And feeling snug doesn't happen only around your belly—remember your legs and thighs, too. This can happen anywhere between the first and the second trimester. Don't let what happened to Cherie happen to you. She was at work during her first pregnancy and was in a company-wide meeting when one of the buyers said, "Cherie, you really look pregnant today. Let's see that cute little belly!" The sound of those words and the image of that conference room send chills down her spine *still*. She giggled and demurred, "It's just a belly, really, it's *too* embarrassing." Well, that was all *this* group needed to hear. The next thing she knew they were all chiming in, "Come on, let's see." At that point, she could tell that the more she pleaded, the more compelling it became for them to get their way. She cut her losses and just got on with inching up her big, loose sweater to expose the top portion of her nonclosing, over-stressed trousers struggling across her bulging belly. To top it off, there were two interlocked safety pins holding the fly closed. She had forgotten that while getting dressed that morning she had grabbed a couple of safety pins off the nearest cleaning bag so that she could wear her favorite trousers one last time. Well, it was one last time all right. As you can imagine, it wasn't a pretty scene.

Pleated trousers. Steer clear. This style pant really does not work once they begin to feel the slightest bit tight. The pleats open up and they don't lay right. Even if you wear them underneath a big tunic sweater, it will be obvious that the fabric is pulling and the pleats aren't pleating. As soon as your tummy begins to grow, which for some people can be as early as seven weeks, fold these up and put them high on a shelf with your tightest jeans.

Drawstring or elastic-waist pants. If you have a lot of these in your closet, you are *golden*. They will be indispensable during the early months of your pregnancy before you start wearing maternity clothes. Without any unnecessary pulling or tugging, they'll be comfortable for many months. But don't fool yourself—they probably won't take you the whole way through your pregnancy (we know, it's hard to imagine that your belly will become too big for expandable pants!). Wide-leg drawstring pants work exceptionally well on taller and/or thinner women.

Stretch fabric pants. Another great pant to move to the front of your closet? Any pant made from the new stretch fabrics (blends of Lycra, nylon, spandex, etc.) that aren't quite leggings but aren't quite pants either. They have elastic waists like leggings, but they give off the look of a pant. These pants are a fairly recent fashion "development" (when we had our kids, pants like these were impossible to find), and we hope you have one or two pairs in your wardrobe. They are great for at least your first and second trimesters.

Leggings

Leggings look great on every pregnant woman, no matter what shape or size you or your legs are. Think about it: Your legs are always going to be smaller than your bulging belly. That's our reasoning, at least. Leggings are the ulti-

mate in comfort, and they're usually made of cotton, which breathes well. You can also dress them up or down depending on what you wear with them. They can take you from day into evening easily with just a quick change of your shoes and accessories. If you have some fun colors or Versace-esque (bold and bright) patterns, these can be great for the start of your pregnancy with a big white T-shirt or solid-color sweater. While you can start off by wearing leggings you already own, in time the tight elastic will become bothersome around your expanding middle. When this happens, it's time to invest in a pair of maternity leggings—one of the single most important pieces of clothing you'll buy. In Chapter 4, we explore the ins and outs of selecting maternity leggings.

Skirts

Not only is a skirt essential for someone who works in the corporate world, but it helps make you feel sexy and feminine, which makes it a *great* choice to wear to a special dinner, too.

If you're lucky enough to have short skirts with elastic waists, these will be perfect. You'll be able to wear them for several months before outgrowing them. Push them to the back of the closet when they become uncomfortable. Knit skirts are a great option, too. These are skirts that are stretchy (usually cotton or cotton blend) and have an elastic band instead of a zipper closure. They'll easily expand with your belly as it grows, giving you more precious time before switching to maternity clothes. Do you have some long knit skirts that you never wear? Now's the time to pull them out. Maybe you have a knit skirt lurking in the back of your closet that came as a set with a matching tunic? When Jody first moved to New York in the eighties, this style was the rage. She had an assortment in a variety of colors and fabrics. If you're a saver, dig into your closet for these. Slim short skirts and long skirts both work really well under a big shirt (but stay away from full skirts—they will make you look like a big frumpy mess). Try your slim skirts on, and if you feel fashionable and good, go for it! When even elastic-waist skirts stop fitting, go directly to the maternity shop. In Chapter 5, we delve deeper into selecting the perfect maternity skirt.

Wearing short black skirts in the summer? We like no hose for a casual look, but it is more slimming if you have a hint of black on your legs to create a fluid look. Think about black Lycra sheer panty hose. But if you're one of those skinny skinnys, go bare and ditch the hose.

If you plan to wear a black short skirt, make sure you wear dark hosiery. A black skirt with black hose creates a very fluid look. Fluid means there appears to be no beginning and end, which helps make you appear thinner (at this point, it's all about illusion!). When we first launched our company, we were guests on a TV talk show where Belly Basics were featured on real pregnant women—sort of an informal fashion show. Always the perfectionists, we spent nearly two hours backstage organizing the clothes before the show aired. We had each outfit numbered, accessorized, and hung all together with the model's name on it. Sound foolproof? We were introduced and they began taping the show, but backstage there was apparently a lot of chaos. The models had just minutes to dress (not good—as we know, pregnant women don't move too fast). Music began blasting, and within seconds the first model was on—in outfit #1: a black tunic and a black skirt. Amid the backstage confusion, she had forgotten to change the cream-colored hose she wore to the studio. She entered the set and it was leg, leg, leg! The outfit was beautifully accessorized with a classic scarf and a stack of tortoise bangle bracelets, but you couldn't help but focus on her legs and only her legs. It wasn't a catastrophe, but it did drive the point home for us (and probably 8 million viewers!) that a black skirt on a pregnant woman looks best with dark hosiery.

Dresses

Now here's a fun category. You should be able to find a few dresses that are just waiting in your closet for you. These might even become your favorites. It has been known to happen. We were casting for our spring brochure recently and a model came to our showroom for a go-see (a quick "size 'em up" interview). She was in her ninth month and was wearing a chocolate brown shirtwaist dress in wool gabardine. She looked fabulous! After we remarked on how great the dress was, she said it was Calvin Klein. She found it at Loehmann's in a size 12 (she's usually an 8) and wore it throughout the pregnancy. A good dress can be a lifesaver. Dresses will work differently for you depending on the season you're currently in, so don't discount anything until you try it on. If it's a dress that fits tightly, think about tying a sweater around your waist to cover the lump in your belly.

As you get a bit bigger, however, you need to be cognizant of how you appear in the dress. We prefer solid-colored dresses with simple lines. Nothing froufrou. No big patterns and certainly no bows (yikes!). It should be a dress that compliments your feminine shape. Many seemingly suitable dresses have way too much material to them, hiding a good portion of your body (this probably sounds good to you, but trust us, it's really not). You end up looking way bigger than you really are. Even if you are big, extra material will make you look positively *jumbo*! For this reason, it is important to pay special attention to the cut of the dress. Make sure it accentuates your positives (yes, you still have some). Does it have a flattering neckline? Do you actually have a shape in the dress or are you, in fact, "all dress"? If you have good legs, show them off ("good" is relative when you're sporting around thirty extra pounds—it really means, do they still look like legs?). If the sleeves of the dress are long, they shouldn't be big and baggy. Check the armhole.

swing

Make sure it's not overly exaggerated. This is not a flattering look. It should fit you closely under the arm. Here are some dress styles that should work throughout most of your pregnancy:

empire-waist

A-line. Literally forms an "A" beginning under your shoulders and continuing to the hem.

Empire-waist. The bodice is slightly more fitted than an A-line. There is a seam underneath the chest, and the dress flairs out slightly from there.

Trapeze/swing. The whole dress swings out from the shoulders down. It's fuller and more "flowy" than either an A-line or an empire-waist—hence the term "swing dress."

A-line

Outerwear

This is the last thing you grab before heading out the door; consequently, it's the last thing you tend to think about. Even for women who aren't pregnant, devoting time, money, and energy to their coats seems last on their seasonal shopping list. But on the contrary, a coat is the one article of clothing you wear repeatedly, day after day, week after week, even season after season. (It's like a pair of glasses—you wear them every single day. They become almost a part of you.) If you are shopping, running errands, or meeting someone outside, a coat is the only piece of clothing everyone really sees. And if you live in a cold climate like Chicago, Boston, or New York, you practically live in your coat.

Have we convinced you yet that a coat is an important wardrobe piece and should be taken quite seriously? Good. Now, let's talk about pregnant women and their coats. We've seen some pretty awful things out there, especially in wintertime. Oddly, some pregnant women seem to think that outerwear is the one area in which they can cheat. Often they wear whatever they wore the season before even though it doesn't fit at all. We liken it to when you're blowing your hair straight and you get to the back and say, "Forget it . . . no one's going to see the back anyway." (Yes, we both have wavy hair and can relate to this.) Well, you happen to be the only person who doesn't see the back of your hair. Kind of like a coat. All we're saying is—at the very least, just make sure it fits. Take a good, long look in the mirror before you dash out the door.

This reminds us of a little tale. We had a lunch meeting on a cold January day with one of our attorneys, who was pregnant. We picked her up at her office to go on to lunch from there. She greeted us looking chic and professional: an Armani-style blazer over a white men's-style shirt, and, of course, a Belly Basics skirt (after all, she is the Belly Basics attorney). Then she grabbed her coat—a long, black wool overcoat. She buttoned the top two buttons and that's as far as she was able to go. Her entire belly was sticking out. We both did a double take and then laughed, assuming this was probably Carol's idea of a little Belly Basics humor. Finally Cherie bravely told her to put her real coat on so we could go. She looked puzzled and said, "This *is* my coat. So I can't button it. I certainly wasn't going to buy a new one." The coat only fit over half of her! New or old isn't the issue at all: a pregnant woman should wear a coat to match the size of her belly.

Thankfully, there are quite a few styles of coats that will work really well on a pregnant body. And most of them are already hanging in your coat closet. You'll be surprised by how many actually can work (almost as surprised by how many *can't*!). Check out the old coats you've refused to part with from years gone by— somehow coats are always harder to get rid of than other clothing. Look through your mom's closet, your sister's or a

tie-front coat

best friend's—one of them might have the right coat hanging around. Last but not least, don't forget your favorite "treasure trove"—your husband's closet. The only coats that really don't work are fitted and structured. Leave them in your closet 'til you look like you again. Here's what works best:

Swing coats. These are a natural. Because they are something of a classic, they may be the easiest to come by.

Tie-front coats. Some of the chicest pregnant women we've seen wear tie-front coats, tying the sash so it rests on *top* of their belly. Tracey, the woman who designed our showroom space, has a brown mohair coat that she wears to work with the sash neatly tied above her belly. The fit is simple. Just move the sash up higher on your belly as you need it.

Duffle coats. Because the fit of these is sort of slouchy anyway, they are comfortable and should work for the duration of your pregnancy.

A-line coats. These may or may not work—the one possible downfall is that they might be too fitted in the chest and belly area. You'll have to try them as you progress to be sure they work.

Parkas. Any down-filled parka should be able to work until delivery day. Their nature is to fit very oversized, and they look really cute over a big belly.

Anorak. These are great. Because of the drawstring, you can pull it tight on top of your belly, under the belly or comfortably loose so it hangs around your belly. Depending on the fabric, they can be great for casual and for slightly dressier occasions.

Men's coats and jackets. The key here is to choose only those coats that are unstructured; otherwise you risk looking like a hobo, being simply smoth-

A-line coat

anorak

ered by a big ole coat! Coats that your husband would wear to work over a suit should probably be off limits (unless of course you and your husband are close to the same size—then they *might* work.) Which styles can work? Try a few on. Cherie's husband, Daniel, had a three-quarter-length duffle coat that she started wearing during her sixth month and continued to wear all winter long. It was a bit overwhelming at the beginning, but as the winter progressed, her belly filled it. She literally wore it every day (Daniel bought a new one). It even made its debut on the first "Serota Baby" tape as Cherie descended the hospital stairs after Stephen was born. Jody found one of David's black casual jackets—she had bought it for him a few years earlier at the Ralph Lauren outlet in Vermont—that was soft, unstructured cotton. With a collar, it had an inside drawstring to tighten or loosen as necessary. Jody wore it all spring and into the summer on cold nights—good thing, too; it was one of those purchases that David never put on his back. Not even once. At least she got some use out of it.

Whew . . . aren't you glad that's over?

We hope you now have a much clearer picture of your pregnancy wardrobe. (Can you believe that you actually already *have* a pregnancy wardrobe?) It should be a relief to find that you do have lots of clothes that will work for you, and to discover that you don't need to go out and spend a week's paycheck on truckloads of maternity clothes. Instead, use the key pieces you unearthed during this chapter to help stretch the few maternity pieces you do buy. In the next chapters, we'll go into greater depth on exactly what those new maternity pieces should be, based on your lifestyle.

The clothes that are in your closet make up the code that unlocks your personal style. They are what you have chosen over the years to dress yourself in, to represent yourself with. They, when taken as a sum of all their parts, are your style. They can't be cast aside now. They are integral to making you feel like you—and making you look like you. Yes, your body is most certainly changing, but your style definitely should not be. It's yours. Don't let anyone—or anything—take it away. Throughout your pregnancy, as you enter each of the various stages, keep this in the forefront of your mind. Pregnancy is a continuation of your life, not a compromise of your style. Even the maternity clothes you buy should fit your own style. There is never cause to let yourself be overtaken by something that's simply not you. Pregnancy is a wondrous, exciting time—watch your belly get big, round, and beautiful and enjoy every minute of it. This is the one thing that woman can do and men never can. Show off your belly—and your style. Be proud of it.

life beyond jeans:
Casual Dressing

Sometimes, the hardest mornings to get dressed happen on days when you're not doing anything special—maybe just running some routine errands, picking up the kids, or dropping off a birthday present at a friend's house. Of course, you always want to look well dressed and "put together," but you just don't feel like expending the energy to get there. For most of us, being a creative dresser takes work. Trying out different options takes time. Envisioning the possibilities with items you already own takes imagination. You want to be able to look in your closet, grab something, and be off.

Here, we'll give you ideas and solutions for just these "non-occasions" as well as for other casual outings when you want to make more of a statement. By planning ahead and strategizing what you'll need before you need it, you'll eliminate the panic and despair of never looking good for the next nine months.

Our friend Randi, a physical therapist from Denver, loves fashion and is constantly reading *Vogue* and *Harper's Bazaar*. One Sunday during her fifth month, she tried to get dressed to go out to a Super Bowl party. Suddenly, nothing fit. She tells of trying on everything "big" in her closet. Within ten minutes, she had created a veritable mountain of discarded clothing. Defeated, she ended up wearing a pair of faded, old leggings (that were uncomfortable because the waistband dug into her belly) and her husband's baggy navy cotton sweater. Needless to say, she wasn't happy with the outcome, especially since her old boyfriend was at the party. Rather than looking pleasantly pregnant, it seemed like she was hiding a few extra pounds.

It's easy to avoid these situations. The first thing you should do is think about the different

Hush Puppies have made a huge resurgence of late, and with good reason, especially for pregnant women. The simple styles come in really fun colors like lilac and hunter green. They are a great legging shoe—either in the classic loafer or in a lace-up. Match your socks to the color of the legging, or wear the shoes without socks during the warmer months. Our friend Daphne, who owns a Manhattan dress shop, had Hush Puppies in three different colors. They became a staple in her everyday wardrobe; she wore a different pair each day with her basic black pregnancy wardrobe. Standing on her feet all day at work, they were perfect—the best way to add a pop of color while incorporating an element of fun!

types of situations for which you'll need to get dressed over the next nine months. Casual dressing is a broad area. It has become the standard for more activities than not. There are so many places and situations where we can dress casually—it is actually the way we both dress most often, day and evening. In fact, there are very few places left in our society where one can't dress casually. Give it a little thought now, and you'll feel much better on days when you have nothing left to squeeze your belly into. Envision your pregnancy in terms of the first part—before your belly begins to pop—and the second part—when it is instantly obvious that your baby is well on the way. When you feel good in your clothing, you exude a different type of outward energy. You appear more confident, which becomes evident in your posture, facial expressions, and even the stride with which you walk (no small trick when you're nine months pregnant!). Consider the woman we met when taking our film to be developed while on a business trip in Miami. She had on heather gray bike shorts, a light pink T-shirt, and a white sweatshirt tied around her shoulders. The T-shirt was untucked, but it was just the right length for the shorts. It was wide enough not to pull across her belly, but not too baggy looking. She wore white Adidas on her

feet, with no socks. She looked terrific. The clothes weren't spectacular; they were the very basic items that we all own. What made her look great was all in the way she pulled it together and, as a result, her outward display of confidence—albeit eight months pregnant.

When your belly is still little

You will probably be able to make do with many of your current clothes until you are into the latter part of your first trimester (although it varies tremendously from one woman to another). The first and most obvious place to start? Your waistband. The key is to accommodate your newly expanding waist without jumping into maternity clothes full force. We must reiterate that during the next nine months you should continue to dress in the style you dressed in before you became pregnant. The clothes you currently own—the ones you fished out during your "closet shopping"—will serve you best at this stage of your pregnancy. Don't run out and buy a whole new wardrobe right now, even though your first temptation is probably to do so. Everything *does* change overnight. You stop drinking coffee. You stop drinking alcohol (although we both had an occasional glass of wine with dinner throughout our pregnancies). You feel suddenly obligated to abstain from your usual morning doughnut, helping yourself instead to a crunchy apple and a large glass of water. But you truly don't need maternity clothes yet. The way you look and feel now is certainly not the way you're going to look or feel a month from now. And you haven't really had enough time to assess your needs.

An attorney named Jackie, who works down the hall from us, came running into our office one morning to announce, "The test was positive! We were up all night rejoicing. It's official. Go ahead. Load me up with your kits!" First we congratulated her. Next we told her to take a deep breath. We sat her down, gave her a cup of coffee (decaf, of course), and told her in no uncertain terms that we would not send her home with The Pregnancy Survival Kit. We wanted her to adjust to her new life—to continue to wear her

own clothes for a few more weeks or maybe even a month. We assured her that nothing would happen overnight and that although she might need to substitute a different pant or skirt with her favorite blazer, her own clothes would work for the next few weeks. Then she could start transitioning her wardrobe. She returned in exactly five weeks. It was time. She was ten weeks pregnant and her skirt was beginning to "dig in." Needless to say, at that point she went home with a kit in every color.

There are a few necessities that will help you get through your first few months, when your belly is still little. We'll start with the one article of clothing a pregnant woman cannot live without.

Leggings

Your own nonmaternity leggings will be your best transitional item as your pants begin tightening around the middle and become harder to button. If this is your first baby, count on wearing these for at least several months (if you're pregnant with your second baby, sometimes your belly pops out immediately and even nonmaternity leggings will feel uncomfortable—you may have to go directly to maternity leggings). Although some people have a hard time believing this, leggings are very slimming because they accentuate the leg. While your belly is growing rapidly bigger and bigger, your legs—no matter what size they are—can't help but look smaller. We once did a segment on a TV talk show in which we made over a pregnant audience member. The girl had very chunky legs and was wearing black pants that were neither full nor slim. Not leggings, just pants. They were very unflattering, and her legs looked very heavy. We put her in a pair of our leggings with a matching tunic. The audience burst into applause at her slim new look. She seemed fifteen pounds thinner. (This is a true story—even now, when we show the tape to friends or family members, they all marvel at the change in her appearance.)

What shoes work with leggings? Boots work best because there are no decisions to make about your socks. If boots aren't appropriate for one reason or another, wear flat shoes or a short,

stacked chunky heel. Never wear a high heel or pump with leggings—pregnant or not. Matching your leggings, shoes, and socks (which will barely peek out from underneath your leggings) will make you appear thinner because you are creating a visual lengthening of your leg.

Pants

Some people seem to live their life in khakis. If you are one of them, don't stop now. Your favorite pants should be a part of your everyday wardrobe as much as possible until you just can't squeeze another day out of them. Our philosophy? Wear tailored clothes at the beginning of your pregnancy to cut down on the time you'll need to wear more typical pregnancy gear. Don't get us wrong, you shouldn't stuff yourself into your normal pants, but you can try to extend their life by using this little trick: Keep a ponytail elastic in your pocket at all times. If things get tight, make a quick escape to the nearest bathroom (which you are probably quite familiar with already), and slip it on as an "extender." Loop the elastic around the button, pull the body of it through your buttonhole, and bring it back over to loop around the button again.

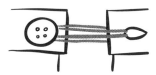

Even this can be stretched out (no pun intended) over several weeks and maybe even months. As your belly gets even bigger and you need even more room, get one of those huge rubber bands (pick them up at any office supply store or take one from your newspaper on Sunday morning) and thread it through the button hole, and wrap it around the button. It'll give your pants lots of extra life. Try not to let the rubber band touch your skin—ouch! Wear a tucked-in T-shirt to protect it. And try to wear a big top over the pants to keep your rubber-band trick a secret. To the casual observer, it should never look as if your pants are just barely making it.

Jeans

A word about your favorite blue jeans: Wear them as much as possible while you still can. Before you know it you'll be yearning for the days when you can fit *anything* into them. At the beginning of your pregnancy you'll most likely be able to wear them regularly, but with each passing week you'll need to make adjustments. At first, just unbutton the top button. When this stops working, try the ponytail-elastic trick. When you can't make your favorite jeans fit any longer (sad, but true . . . it will happen), you can always try one of our favorite things—wearing your husband's jeans. Cinch the waist with a belt. Jody wore David's Levi's with a tucked-in T-shirt underneath an unbuttoned flannel shirt to a Sunday afternoon "season opener" football party. The jeans made her look as if she had sort of a potbelly rather than a pregnant belly. It takes a certain amount of confidence to pull this off. The people there knew her and knew her regular size, so it was fun for her to wear something different.

Jeans are sexy on a pregnant woman when worn with a bodysuit or close-fitting top. As we all know, by now your breasts are tremendous and very sexy. (Even our skinny friend Kim, who was a 32A before she was pregnant, graduated to a 36C by week four.) While your belly is still little you should flaunt them—something you might not do under normal circumstances. Being pregnant seems to give you carte blanche to play this up. Your hormones are in full swing, and you might feel a little more daring than usual. We saw a woman in a Florida mall during one of our spring events who did just this. She was a blonde in her early twenties, approximately five months pregnant. She was wearing a pair of hip-hugging jeans, which hit her right under her pregnant belly, with a halter tank top. Her entire belly was "hanging out." Now that may be a little too daring for some of us, but at least she didn't change her personal style just because she was pregnant!

If you wear jeans religiously this may be a maternity purchase you want to make. Here is what to look for:

Style of leg. Buy the same type of jean leg you wore before you became pregnant (i.e., boot leg versus slim leg). The leg is really all anyone is going to see—more than likely you'll cover the top portion of your jeans with a shirt.

If you are a devoted jeans person and can't see yourself going through nine months without your favorite pair, think about creating your own special "maternity" jeans. Buy a maternity panel from a notions store and take it to a tailor and have it sewn into your jeans. They'll fit comfortably over your belly as it continues to grow. Our friend Liora, a swimwear designer, did this with two pairs of jeans during her pregnancy and was never without them. One pair had frayed bottoms and was totally worn in, and the other pair was white. We were all used to seeing her in both of them so she still seemed like herself. One thing to consider if you're going to do this is whether or not you can sacrifice your favorite jeans to this cause. Remember, there's no turning back. Once you turn your jeans into maternity jeans, you'll never be able to wear them as regular jeans again.

Pockets and stitching that look as close to your favorite nonmaternity jeans as possible.

Fabric. A finish that you are used to wearing—stonewashed, dark blue, faded, etc.

A comfortable fit. The jeans will probably have some sort of panel at the top. We prefer side panels or concealed side elastic instead of the front panel. This way you can wear a shirt tucked in during the beginning months without it looking odd. And the jeans will grow as you grow.

Denim overalls

We should start by saying that if you are over 5′7″ tall, our recommendation is that you not wear denim overalls, whether you're pregnant or not. Have you ever seen a tall person look good in overalls? Have you ever actually seen a tall person in overalls? Probably not many. The proportions don't seem to work. Anyway, if you meet the height criterion, this is a great look while you are still at the beginning of your pregnancy. Overalls fit baggy anyway, and no one will notice the extra bulge around your waist as it hides under overalls. Try wearing them with the following:

Simple turtlenecks. This is a great chance to wear the ribbed turtlenecks that you'll otherwise be hard-pressed to wear. Even though they'll be fitting tightly across your belly, your belly is hidden so it doesn't matter. You'll be showing off the parts of your body that are still slender—your arms, your neck, your collarbones. We love this look. The other kind of turtleneck that will work is a basic "ski" turtleneck. Whether it's yours or your husband's, you'll be comfortable in it. It's a baggier look than a tight ribbed turtleneck. Just know the effect you'll be achieving—more of a functional look, like you're dressed for cold weather. A close-fitting turtleneck creates a trendier look.

Sweaters. A thin sweater—whether it's cotton, wool, silk, or rayon—looks cool under jean overalls. As long as the sweater isn't too bulky, there's an endless variety of necklines that will work. Ideally the sweater should have a wide bottom so that it hangs well and easily. But try a few of your sweaters on. Even if they don't have a wide bottom, they could work. It depends both on where the sweater hits you and how your overalls fit.

Shoes with overalls: a lace-up work boot is one of the best looks because it's the most authentic—it has that vague farmer feeling. But any kind of heavy shoe will work, i.e., clogs, heavy loafers, ankle boots. Just don't wear a shoe meant for the office. You don't want to wear a feminine-looking shoe with overalls. A major fashion "don't" for anyone—pregnant or not.

Long-sleeved shirts. A very casual look that's great because it shows off the shape of your body under the overalls (if the shirt is tight fitting).

Thermal shirts. Perfect under overalls because they're close fitting, which complements the baggy overalls. Plus the waffle knit will stretch easily over your growing belly. It's also the ultimate in comfort.

Sweatpants

Our feelings on this subject are short and sweet: Don't even *think* of leaving the house in your sweats. We know the temptation is sometimes there, say on a rainy Sunday when you're not really going anywhere. Resist it. Sweatpants should be worn out only if you're heading for the gym. Other than that, they shouldn't leave the house. They are unflattering, sloppy, and give off a distinct aura of having given up on style. In a word, yuck!

Shorts

Try wearing any of your elastic-waist shorts—that includes, naturally, yours and your husband's. Without going to a store, first check your own drawers (if you didn't do this while "closet shopping"). You probably have a few shorts with a drawstring or an elastic waist. Even if they aren't your favorites, they will be perfect for the first half of your pregnancy. You can always wear them with a big white T-shirt and a pair of sandals or, depending on the fabric and style of the shorts, gym shoes. After you've thoroughly exhausted your own supply, it's time to move on. Go directly to your husband's stash. Our friend Meryl found an entire stack of "gym shorts" that were all perfect for running around. There was one black pair of gym shorts—you know, the rayon kind with the tiny "holes" in the fabric—that she wore constantly with a big white T-shirt and Tevas (those sport sandal/shoes with Velcro straps that have become all the rage). On a trip to San Diego, she realized that her bike shorts were just too hot and she hadn't packed any other shorts. She looked through her husband's suitcase, and, by some stroke of luck, he had packed those black gym shorts. If you're lucky enough to stumble across a pair of these athletic shorts, wear them with a big T-shirt. Crewneck T-shirts, V-necks, or polo necks all work well with this type of short. Stick to a gym shoe (or Tevas, Birkenstocks, etc.) on your feet.

Your husband's walking shorts

This might sound funny to you, and indeed it is pretty funny in retrospect for us to think that David's shorts—made for a guy 6'3"—and Daniel's shorts—made for a guy 5'10"—could fit Jody and Cherie respectively. But they did. When your belly is little, say maybe the third

through fifth or sixth month, try slipping on a pair of men's khaki walking shorts. All guys have these somewhere in their drawers. They'll definitely be too big on you, so belt the waist tightly across your belly. They should fit over your expanding abdomen. Experiment with them on a day when you have some spare time. You might *love* the look—we certainly do. If not, don't give up before you try them on with:

Your husband's polo shirts. When Jody was pregnant and just starting to get a belly over the summer, she loved wearing David's khaki shorts, his brown woven belt (it was easy . . . no notches to fit into!), and his big polo shirts. They're just what you'd wear *non*pregnant on a summer weekend day or a casual summer night. (They were also perfect for the golf course, a place where it seems Jody hasn't returned since having a baby. Eighteen holes? Forget it, where's the baby going to go? They don't make golf "car seats." Hey, now there's an idea!)

With your own T-shirts. Wear your T-shirt tucked into the shorts—it needn't be a jumbo-size shirt. In fact, a tight-fitting little

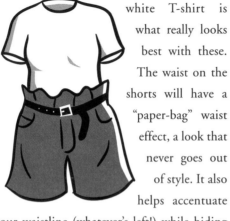

white T-shirt is what really looks best with these. The waist on the shorts will have a "paper-bag" waist effect, a look that never goes out of style. It also helps accentuate your waistline (whatever's left!) while hiding your newly rounded belly.

A white cotton button-down shirt. Try tying it up at your waist! Well, actually, since you don't really have a waist any longer, the tie will fit around the actual waistline of the shorts, rather than above it. This look takes a certain amount of confidence to wear, but if you've got someplace in particular to go, it's a terrific look that's very clean and crisp. But (we're not *completely* off the wall) you can only wear a shirt tied at the waist while your tummy is still fairly little. You'll know when this stops working for you. When it does, try wearing the shirt open as a "jacket."

Drawstring/elastic-waist pants

You are going to be *so* happy slipping these awesome pants on each morning. They are so comfortable, you'll want to sleep in them. The best news? They look like regular pants because they *are* your regular pants (sounds a bit obvious, but sometimes these things need to be said).

Boxer shorts

If you want to wear these out somewhere, take a good long look in the mirror first. Are they long enough to cover your thighs? Is the flap going to open up when you sit down, revealing your underwear for all to see? If you love the fit of one or two pairs and they look good enough to wear out in public, sew down the front flap so you don't have to worry about it opening while you're out and about. Just check periodically (every two weeks or so) in the mirror to make sure they are still covering what they're supposed to be covering.

We hope you were able to dig some up from your own closet. You'll be able to wear these for at least the first trimester and probably well into your second. The drawstring pant is great, because it's an almost magical concept for a pregnant woman—as you continually grow, it continually grows! We don't suggest purchasing a pair specifically for your pregnancy, though, unless you think you'll wear them when you're done. They won't take you as far along as you might think they will. On a recent Saturday, we ran into a fashion editor while at Bloomingdale's doing an event. Coincidentally, she was five months pregnant. She was wearing a chocolate brown Belly Basics top and fabulous silk drawstring pants. We complimented her on how terrific she looked and she laughed and recounted the story of how she had purchased them on a whim one day a couple of years ago from a J. Crew outlet; they were the type that had been marked down twice and looked like they'd been tried on by half the world. Well, they ended up sitting in her closet unworn with the tag still

attached. Every time she put them on, she felt they were too big and too baggy. Then she got pregnant. As soon as her belly began to grow a little, she thought of them and pulled them out.

Try wearing elastic-waist pants with:

A white Hanes T-shirt. The favorite standby.

Tank tops worn tucked in. (This works only if the pant has a drawstring waist— if it's just elastic, it looks wrong.) The combination is perfect when it's really hot, and can look great if you're in good shape (if your arms have gotten heavy already, stay away from tank tops). When your belly is still little, it works beautifully. If you want to spruce it up a little, try wearing a metal I.D. or dog tag necklace, which works especially well with a classic tank top. If you're wearing a beaded necklace, wear only one strand, because when it's hot, too many strands around your neck can be uncomfortable.

A loose blouse or button-down shirt. This is a great transitional look as your belly really begins to grow but you haven't yet graduated to real maternity clothes.

What should you wear on top of your jeans, khakis, leggings, and pants?

Sweaters

The perfect thing to toss on with a pair of leggings. Any color will work as long as the style is right. You'll probably end up with two or three favorites that you toss on most days without a second thought. Easy and simple. Effortless. As long as the fit is good, who needs to stand in front of a closet searching and thinking? The rules are simple: If you want to wear a sweater with your leggings or any other pant that perhaps isn't closing all the way, make sure it's a tunic sweater (one with a wide bottom). If it has a tight ribbed bottom, it's not a tunic sweater and it is meant to be worn with good-fitting jeans or slacks. It's probably going to look wrong with leggings or extended-life khakis. The ribbed bottom will hug your legs and give even the skinniest of women a universally unattractive pear shape. If you have a sweater that's not a tunic but is something you think will work, just try it on and check the fit every few weeks. What worked at week twenty-four might not work at week twenty-six. Take a second to look in the mirror from all angles. Sit down. Make sure the sweater doesn't ride up. If it does, don't wear it—you'll be fooling with it all day.

Most of us already own a tunic sweater that will work. Even if you can find only one or two in your closet, you'll be fine. You can wear that one sweater a million different ways. Try these looks:

- with a white T-shirt underneath
- with a contrasting color T-shirt underneath
- with a turtleneck
- with a collared shirt—preferably white
- belted with a medium-width belt (1½ to 2

inches wide). This depends on the size of your belly and the fabric of the sweater. It works only if the sweater is a fine-gauge knit like silk, "cotton cashmere," lightweight wool, lightweight cashmere, etc. It will be too bulky to work this way if it's a heavier knit.

Cardigans

A cardigan sweater is great because it is an easy, casual alternative to a blazer or jacket. It's less structured so it's more comfortable. It creates a layered look (our favorite) which results in more of an outfit rather than just separate pieces worn together. And from a practical standpoint, it can be a pregnant woman's best friend—frequent bouts with hormonal temperature swings will be a regular occurrence for you. Slip it on and off with ease. If the cardigan is long enough and it's early enough in your pregnancy, you can even belt it with a leather belt (a medium-width belt with a chunky metal buckle looks great cinched around a sweater for a sporty look). A cardigan works well with leggings, jeans, or khaki pants.

When Cherie was pregnant she absolutely lived in a black V-neck cardigan. She wore it as a blazer alternative, or layered over either a button-down oxford or T-shirt on top of her leggings. One evening when she was five months pregnant she wore this favorite combo of hers to a casual business dinner. At Daniel's request, she vowed not to tell their dinner partners that she was pregnant (not everyone in his office knew yet and he wanted to be the one to tell them). With the help of this concealing sweater, she managed to keep it a secret all evening. But by the middle of dessert, Daniel looked over at Cherie, who was feasting on a double chocolate mousse cake, and couldn't help but blurt out their news, "A few more pieces like that and the baby's going to come out licking his lips!" (Men— they *are* the weaker sex, aren't they!)

Jody's pine green, classic men's cardigan (it originally belonged to David) served a totally different purpose. She'd wear a tight white T-shirt underneath and button just one button of the sweater, in the middle or so. It was perfect for just running around. It was comfortable and easy to toss on, but it also showed some of her body so she didn't feel like a total slob. Even now, she frequently finds herself tossing it on in the early morning as she juggles a crying baby and a toddler demanding juice—all three of them standing in the doorway of her little closet.

Assorted knit shirts

Long or short-sleeved knit shirts of any type are great as long as they are long enough to cover your midsection.

Turtlenecks of any fabric are great, but be wary of tight knits at this point in your pregnancy. If you're the type of person who likes to show off her figure as much as possible, this is an awkward time. It's a little weird to wear something tight because you don't really look pregnant. While we definitely advocate showing off your belly, the beginning months leave you looking far more like you need to tighten

your abdominals than like you've actually got a baby in there. At this stage, stick to tops that don't hug your little pouch.

Vests

A big vest in a solid color is invaluable for a pregnant woman. It looks great worn with pants and leggings and—good news—a nonmaternity vest could actually make it throughout your entire pregnancy. The other day at Jody's play group, one of the mothers, Sharon, who had had two children in rapid succession, walked in with a garment in a dry-cleaning bag and handed it to Tobin, who was pregnant with her second baby. It was a black corduroy vest (nonmaternity) that Sharon had lived in for both her pregnancies. The inside had a classic black-watch plaid lining. It was casual and comfortable, yet something a little different than a sweater. Notwithstanding the fact that Sharon is 5′9″ and a size 10 and Tobin is 5′4″ and a size 6, the vest looked equally good on both of them. Because of this size adaptability, it's a great item to borrow. Cherie's next-door

When your belly is still little:

For a different look, try tucking your shirt into your pants, provided you wear something to cover the waistband (which by now is probably completely or partially unzipped). Try covering your waistband with these:

• A thin wool sweater tied around your waist. The bulk from the sweater and the knot will cover up your waist and take away emphasis. (This is not a look for leggings!)

• An oversized cardigan. You can wear it completely buttoned up or with only the top button fastened to keep the sweater from flapping open. This way you can still show some waist.

• A vest. It has to be the perfect shape—wide at the bottom, big enough armholes, a V-neck, preferably in a nice deep color.

neighbor borrowed a charcoal gray sweatshirt vest from her coworker on Wall Street and wore it all the time on the weekends. If you

can't find one to borrow, think about picking one up in the large-size shop of any department store or discount store (look for size XL).

Denim shirts

A denim shirt is pretty much a can't-live-without item. It doesn't matter whose it is—yours or your husband's. Just make sure it's long enough to cover your butt and thighs, otherwise it will look like you're only half dressed—like you either forgot the shirt that's supposed to go over it, or you forgot to put on your pants. This is why it's usually better to take your husband's during your pregnancy. Like a cardigan, it can be fully buttoned or it can be left open to show some more of your body. Wear it casually with any kind of T-shirt shirt underneath. This is definitely a matter of what you feel comfortable in and is a reflection of your pre-pregnancy style. Jody's sister-in-law Lauren, a stay-at-home mom in New Jersey, virtually lived in a soft denim shirt during her pregnancy. She always wore it fully buttoned. It wasn't even an issue for her. A denim shirt happens to work really well with a black pair of leggings, too. And as your belly grows and you near the end of your pregnancy, you can continue to wear it—a definite bonus. Just open it up, jacket style, over a cotton maternity tunic top. It's a comfortable look that you'll feel comfortable *in*. A denim shirt, for some reason we've yet to figure out, has gained a universal acceptance as appropriate dress for almost all situations—from running to the grocery store to having a casual dinner out. It even looks great under a blazer (à la Ralph Lauren) with a scarf wrapped around your neck. And the beauty of it is that denim shirts are meant to be full and baggy, so they are bound to fit throughout most of your pregnancy. Another great feature? The more you wash them, the softer they get. Once in Nashville, during our seasonal fashion show on national TV, one of our models was slated to wear our black tunic and leggings with a big

blazer over a denim
shirt with a scarf

denim shirt for a casual daytime look. Well, oops, the blue denim shirt that the stylist had chosen was way too short for the tunic, which hung out from the back like a flag. We had about sixty seconds to correct the situation before taping. Out of the corner of her eye, Jody spotted our producer sitting innocently in front of a monitor wearing none other than a denim shirt (nicely worn in, too). We literally took the shirt right off his back and threw it on our pregnant model. A perfect fit!

One final word. Your husband, if he's anything like Cherie's, may be very attached to his favorite denim shirt—the one that he throws on for his early-Sunday-morning outings to get the bagels and the newspaper. Tell him to get over it—that shirt has rightfully become yours. For all the sweat and tears (not to mention bloating) you have to withstand during pregnancy, he should just wear a sweatshirt on

Sunday mornings and pray that you don't swipe anything else from his closet.

When your belly pops

Every woman starts to show at a different point in her pregnancy. No one can predict exactly when your belly is going to pop. It does depend a lot on your body type and whether or not you have been pregnant before. But do be forewarned—you can't dictate the way you're going to carry. Besides eating correctly, there's little you can do to change your fate. And as we've said before, even if you eat right, your body is going to do exactly what it wants (easy for us to say, sitting back with our pre-baby bellies). Because of the nature of our business, and because it seems as if either one or the other of us is always pregnant, we have seen it all. On the weekends and during the work-week, not a day passes when we don't see pregnant women. We can assure you—very few of them carry as they expected to. Some start to show on week six and others keep it hidden for six months. Some carry in front and others just get wider around their middle. Whatever your shape, you'll need to be more creative as your options become more limited.

Casual wear: what to buy

There are some essential items you'll need to invest in now that you've started to show. These are core items, the basics, the pieces you can wear everyday. Once you have the maternity basics, which work especially well if they are black or a neutral color (navy, brown, sand), you simply layer on items from your very own closest.

Here are the casual essentials: 1) leggings, 2) a simple tunic, and 3) a basic dress.

1. Leggings

Essential! Yes, it's true. At some point, you're going to have to succumb to reality and invest in a pair of specially designed maternity leggings. Regular leggings leave no room for your belly to grow. The elastic becomes too tight across your belly, causing, among other things, a big stomachache. Your belly gets bigger at the end of the day, and, compounded with your just-eaten dinner or lunch, the last thing you want to do is wear constricting clothing. When Jody was pregnant with her second baby, at just seven weeks she started wearing maternity leggings. Because it had not been that long since her first pregnancy (her kids are nineteen months apart), her belly immediately popped and regular leggings were uncomfortable—the elastic dug like hell into her belly. On New Year's Eve she was in Colorado and was getting dressed to go to a New Year's party. Suddenly, nothing worked anymore. Her regular pants wouldn't close, so she ended up wearing her Banana Republic leggings—her last resort. Needless to say, while they served their purpose—she was able to go to the party—they were horribly uncomfortable. Two days later, she was glad to be home in New York, where she slipped into good ole Belly Basics leggings for the duration of her pregnancy. Look for a pair of basic leggings in black—quite simply the most versatile piece of clothing ever made.

Pick your waistband. There are a lot of different waistbands out there—almost as many as there are body types—and everyone has her own preference. We are both partial to a nonelastic waistband, which for us was by far the most comfortable, and so, naturally, that's how we designed our own legging. We call it "The Ultimate Legging" because we truly feel it is. The leggings stay up without elastic because the cotton/Lycra is sewn as a four inch-wide "panel" that hugs your belly. When we were pregnant we found that the other leggings we tried would get progressively more uncomfortable as the day went on. We happily ditched the elastic. During Cherie's first pregnancy (pre–Belly Basics) she couldn't find leggings that didn't dig into her belly. Many times she would grab the closest pair of scissors (one time she had to ask the waitress for a pair while she was out to dinner) and cut the elastic band. It was always such a relief. Cherie tried a lot of different leggings in search of the perfect pair, saying repeatedly, "If only I knew how to sew!" Well, the story goes like this: Cherie didn't know how to sew, and neither did Jody, but in New York City it's not hard to find somebody who does. We trudged our way up eight floors of a walk-up on Thirty-eighth Street and Seventh Avenue to visit a sample maker named Sandy. As we stood in a smoke-filled room, our conversation with her seemed more like a game of charades than a business meeting. Since we didn't know "shop talk" at that point, we pulled out about four pairs of leggings and showed the sample maker what worked, what didn't work, and why. We tried on each pair, and, like stirring a "witches' brew," she took our concoction of leggings and our few amateur sketches and together we created the perfect pair of leggings, our Ultimate Legging. Its four-inch panel fits snugly on your tummy, without digging or pinching, and grows as you grow. Leggings really are the perfect pant alternative for the pregnant woman. One of our goals when we founded Belly Basics was to create cool-looking clothes that were comfortable

(what a novel idea). In fact, even nonpregnant, we both *still* wear our Belly Basics leggings.

Some women prefer other waistbands. There is one style with an elastic waistband that sits on top of your belly. They look just like a regular pair of leggings but were created with extra room in the belly. Another popular waistband rests below your belly, letting it all hang out. This is definitely not for everyone, but some women swear by it. Do some research on your own. Talk to friends and try on a few different pairs. Make sure you find the style that you're most comfortable wearing. Trust us, by the time your belly is visibly sticking out, a pair of great-fitting leggings will become indispensable.

2. A black tunic

Essential! Think of this as the most versatile piece of clothing in any chic woman's wardrobe. The options are endless. It goes with almost anything, but we like it best worn simply with black leggings. Refreshingly easy to wear and exceptionally slimming, it's part of an effortless outfit that you'll always look good in. Don't limit yourself to this combination, though. Be creative. The delight of a solid tunic (especially in black) is that if you continually change your accessories, you change the look of the tunic.

Here's what to look for when shopping for that classic, essential tunic:

Very simple styling. Keep in mind that the more simple the design, the more versatile the tunic. Don't buy something with fancy stitching, decorations, any type of buttons or bows, and expect it to be your versatile wardrobe anchor. Clean and simple is best. The tunic we designed for The Pregnancy Survival Kit met our strict criteria, plus it had a flattering round neckline to show off pretty collarbones while allowing our bulging bellies room to move.
Good fit. It should drape loosely over your belly.
Natural fabrics. The fabric should be a natural fiber, one that lets you breathe.
Easy cleaning. Check to make sure it's machine

One easy way to give your tunic a totally different look is by wearing a collared shirt underneath. Slip on one of your regular blouses so that the collar peeks out from the neckline. As long as you can button a few of the top buttons, the rest can remain unbuttoned. Try folding your shirt cuffs up, too. This helps change the look of the tunic into more of a layering piece, serving the same function as a crewneck sweater. It's still a casual look but more styled—like you actually took a little more time in your heartburn-filled morning.

washable. It will make your life a lot easier. When you wear a shirt more than twice a week (which, believe us, you will), you can't afford not to have it around while it awaits its turn at the dry cleaner.

3. A great dress
Essential! A dress can be fabulous for a variety of occasions from ultra-laid-back to dressy events. You just have to have the right one. It does need to fit you in a few key places, which,

as we all know, can be quite different from one woman to another. It shouldn't pull across the chest or the back or be so tight that you can see bra strap marks in back (what we have termed "back fat"). It's tough to find nonmaternity dresses—especially in the winter—that will make it all the way through your nine months. You'll most likely end up purchasing a maternity dress. Black is our personal favorite because it's so versatile and basic. You absolutely could wear it wherever you go—we know because we did. A black dress—provided it's simple—is not the type of thing someone might remember you having worn. What they might remember is how good you looked when you wore it. Choose a solid color for more versatility, and one that works with comfortable shoes you know you'll be wearing often. When we first introduced The Pregnancy Survival Kit, like Henry Ford with his first Model T car,

we offered it in black only. But we met many customers who said they just didn't feel right in black. As two New Yorkers who own a ton of black, we were utterly shocked. But the next season we decided to offer our dress in other colors. It was a huge success. Every person has somewhat of a signature palette that they lean toward. Go with your gut. During our winter pregnancies, we both lived in our Belly Basics black cotton/Lycra dress.

Our Belly Basics dress, what we call "Our Favorite Dress," is *just* that. It has a subtle empire waist, a flattering "bodysuit" neckline, and a sleeve that fits close to your arm. Because it is nearly Zen-like in its simplicity, it's inherently easy to dress it up or down. And after seeing it on all types of women—huge, tiny, and everything in between—we can honestly say it *is* the quintessential maternity dress. Again, we think a comfortable, machine-washable fabric like a cotton/Lycra is the best. Eliminate the dry cleaner. Another important feature of cotton/Lycra is that it can be worn totally casually or, just as easily, more dressed up (which we will go into more detail about in Chapter 7). Once when we visited Bloomingdale's in California for a Belly Basics event, the store manager greeted us with bounding enthusiasm. We were psyched; usually we get a "Hi. Great to have you. Gotta run. I'm late to a meeting" greeting. This particular store manager, Casey, had given birth only two months before to a little boy named Rex. She proceeded to tell us how she lived in Belly Basics, wearing a piece of it almost every day. She then dragged us to her office. On her desk she had a framed picture of the department Christmas party (a casual bash at a local Mexican joint). It was a group shot of about twenty people. She had on our simple dress in chocolate brown with an equestrian-motif scarf that incorporated blue, yellow, and cream. She wore brown opaque hosiery and a dark coffee (almost black) shoe. Casey looked fabulous. A great dress will do it for you. We know, it sometimes seems much easier to throw on leggings and a big sweater, but for a casual

occasion a simple dress is a truly effortless outfit that's always a winner.

The summer dress

When you're really pregnant during the summer and you're lugging around a huge belly in the heat, an easy dress is a natural. And lucky for you, nonmaternity dresses are easy to find in the summer (there had to be *some* payoff to being pregnant when it's sweltering outside). Here are our thoughts on this subject. While it will seem like nearly every dress will make it though nine months, there are some caveats. First, you should consider a nonmaternity dress only if you are a

How to hem a maternity dress: It's easy if you keep in mind that maternity dresses are designed to be slightly longer in front than in back. If the dress was designed for maternity, have the tailor (or yourself if you are handy) take off the same amount—e.g., two inches—all around rather than hemming it so that it lies flat front to back. If the dress is nonmaternity, make sure the tailor leaves at least a quarter inch more length in the front than in the back.

fairly small size to begin with. Otherwise the front of your dress will start to hike up as your belly gets bigger (which can actually happen anyway even if you are a size 2). This looks ridiculous and is the main reason most women resort to buying maternity anyway. But don't misunderstand—it *can* work. The dress must be constructed with enough fabric so that when your belly begins to take up more than its allotted share, it can be accommodated. A short-sleeved dress is the easiest style to wear, especially if you're on the bigger size. Another great style to consider is a sleeveless dress that can be worn really casually or, quite easily, a little more dressy. If you are happy with the way your arms look (don't be too critical), a sleeveless dress is the best way to play them up, and believe us, when your belly is bulging, you'll want to play up anything you can.

If you do plan on purchasing a nonmaternity dress, take into consideration that you will need to go up at least a size or two. A tank dress is meant to be full and is an easy dress for a pregnant woman to wear. A swing dress is

another perfect style for a pregnant woman. But stay away from bold patterns—they won't work. Bows and even buttons on this type of dress are also too cutesy and predictable. But when it's right . . . Cherie's sister-in-law Diana once came up to our office wearing a flowing rayon dress in a soft, neutral, ditzy print (inside fashion term for tiny, tiny little flowers). She wore it with brown woven sandals and looked strikingly like Daisy Buchanan in *The Great Gatsby*—totally classic and very feminine.

Here are other casual pieces that will mix in with your essentials and help stretch your nine-month wardrobe:

Casual pants

If you are the type of person who follows the trends and likes to look the most current you possibly can, there *is* a way to be trendy and pregnant. Go to a discount store or a junior department where the prices are affordable. Purchase a pair of the "in" pants of the season (e.g., not long ago it was the bell bottom, now it's the boot leg). Go to your local notions store and pick up a maternity panel (the same tech-nique we suggested for your jeans). They sell them in every color—we know they are not the height of fashion, but they'll definitely make any pair of pants work for you. Have a seam-stress sew it in for you. Keep in mind that pants with back or side zips will work a little better. When bell bottoms were the rage, our friend Margie, a copywriter at an entertainment mag-azine, had her standard outfit for casual nights out with friends: black silk/gabardine bell bot-toms and a black tunic top. She looked terrific and never looked like she was wearing typical maternity clothes.

Remember to save the piece that the seam-stress cuts out. Depending on the fabric, it sometimes can be put right back in after your baby is born—and you'll have your pants back.

Wide-legged pants

Some women just feel more comfortable in looser clothes. While wide-legged maternity pants are certainly comfortable, they can make you appear larger. So beware and try not to wear

an exaggerated palazzo pant—unless, of course, you're tall and pencil-slim to begin with.

Riding pants

Cherie's play group unanimously agreed that riding pants were their favorite when they were pregnant (riding pants are a legging with a slightly wider leg, made out of a spandex/ nylon, with decorative suede patches on the inside of the knees). They all liked this type of pant because it achieved the same purpose as leggings: making their legs look thin. Yet it was a dressier alternative, a bit more tailored and perhaps more classic. They also liked the flexi-bility of having something that was as com-fortable as a tried-and-true legging, but that offered a totally different look. Chocolate brown is a great color for a riding pant. Classic and slimming. Sand is also a great color, but it may make your legs look heavier. Whatever color you choose, a riding pant always looks great with a white button-down shirt. You can look for this type of pant in a more upscale maternity shop, but if you can't find one that has the right detailing (sometimes that's what's lacking in maternity items) buy a regular pair you love (make sure it contains Lycra) and either sew in the panel or buy them a few sizes too big. It's not an item you have to spend a lot of money on, either. You can probably find a pair at The Limited or any other trendy store. Or go to an equestrian shop and get an authentic pair (these will definately cost more). They are pretty stretchy and will probably work most of the way through your pregnancy.

Bike shorts

You definitely need to leave any preconceived notions about bike shorts back in the first trimester. Whatever you may or may not have thought about them, they will be a lifesaver as your belly grows large and the humidity and heat start to get to you. We do agree that if you're not pregnant, bike shorts belong only in a gym. But when you are pregnant, this is the one exception we allow—the fashion police won't come looking for you! You should really invest in a pair—probably in black, at least to

start. Just like with the leggings, the special fit is crucial to accommodate your growing belly. A maternity bike short will give you the room you need where you need it. Again, we recommend a pair with a nonelastic waistband—this is particularly crucial for the hot months because you don't want anything like elastic contributing to your discomfort. During Jody's second pregnancy (she delivered on August 5) she had two pairs of bike shorts that she lived in (by the way, she is someone who would normally *never* wear bike shorts off the Stairmaster). One was black and the other was a neutral sand color. For running around with her two-year-old daughter, there was nothing easier. When it got really hot she wore them with a matching big tank top, or otherwise, just a simple XL Hanes T-shirt in white. Bike shorts can actually be flattering, and can even look stylish when worn with the same color top. We're not talking Gyranimals here, but a solid-colored top with a matching bike short is always more slimming than two colors mixed (let's not even *discuss* patterns). It's easy to wear because you don't feel "head-to-toe color" as you might in a bright top and leggings. This is a great alternative to wearing a summer cotton dress, and, to some people, it's more comfortable. Why? There's no need to worry about your underwear showing or the back of your legs sticking to vinyl seats in a greasy diner or a dirty taxicab. It's an easy, casual way of looking pulled together. Don't think you have to wear strictly gym shoes with bike shorts either. They work with sandals and even flat loafers, depending on the look you're going for. Any type of footwear can work with bike shorts as long as it doesn't have a heel. *That* won't work.

A full-length unitard

This is a great way to show off your belly if you're one of those few skinny pregnant women who look like they swallowed a basketball (don't we all wish). It also makes a great first layer of clothing for all body types. Simply wear a large button-down shirt over it—a denim shirt always works. A blazer over a unitard is another great look. It's very slenderizing because you're not wearing a lot of extra clothing, which will eliminate bulk under the blazer.

The unitard needn't be maternity, just one size larger if it's stretchy enough. Check out the hosiery department and ask the sales associates—most do have some unitards. Two nights before Jody's first baby was born she went to dinner with her college roommates. She wore a black unitard with an oversized blue velvet shirt on top and closed just the top button. At one point, when she went to the bathroom and her three friends joined her (why do college friends always go to the bathroom together, even fifteen years later?), they made her take off her shirt so they could get a better look at her belly. They touched her, turned her around to get side views, felt the baby kicking, and basically freaked out—it was a truly memorable girlfriend-bonding moment. But

here's the caveat: One big drawback to wearing a unitard is not only having to pull down the top of the unitard when you go to the bathroom, but also having to remove whatever you've worn on top of it. And when you go to the bathroom every seven minutes or so, this can be a big bummer.

Skirts

For casual occasions the most comfortable skirts are made out of cotton/Lycra. Long or short, both work depending on your preference. A skirt should reach your ankles if it's long, and should definitely be straight. Full skirts look dowdy and will make you look even bigger than you are. A skirt looks better if there's some definition from the belly on down, even on somebody with very heavy legs.

A big shirt

At this point, most of your own blouses will be too small to fit properly over your belly. Don't try to squeeze. Not only will you have a hard time buttoning them, but they'll end up

being too short to cover your bum. Wearing your husband's shirts is one of the best ways to stretch your maternity wardrobe without investing any money. Jody used to remove David's briefly worn shirts from the night before right off the closet door. They were still crisp and clean (assuming he didn't spill red wine or tomato sauce), but they were just a little softer than if you took them straight from the closet and their dry-cleaning bag. And she didn't have to stand there thinking about which shirt to choose from his vast selection. For knocking around the house or running errands, wear leggings with one of his oversized flannel shirts. Or try his classic patterned dress shirts (stripes, men's wear patterns, etc.) and crisp white shirts. These can look really chic if the fit is right on you, but you're the only one who can be a judge of that (of course, best friends do come in handy for this type of thing). When trying on his shirts, make sure that the hem of the shirt isn't hitting your knees—not a good look at all. On the other hand, you must make sure your thighs are covered. Keep in mind that not every shirt will work, and not everybody can fit into her husband's shirts. It depends on your size in relation to his size, what you're comfortable wearing, and even your lifestyle. What might look terrific on a woman who is a size 6 at 5′4″ could look rotten on a size 10 at 5′8″—or vice versa. If you feel comfortable wearing them, they'll become staples in your wardrobe to wear out to dinner, to see friends, or to go pretty much anywhere. However, if you just don't feel right in his shirts, pick up a maternity shirt.

Though white shirts are our personal favorites, there's one caveat about white—think twice if you already have a child at home and you'll be spending the day with him or her. No matter how hard you try to stay clean, it's virtually impossible. Our friend Deni once put on her favorite classic men's white shirt to go out to dinner and the movies with her husband, Larry. After sitting and playing with her sixteen-month-old and feeding him dinner, there was tomato sauce smeared on the back of the shirt—in the pattern of little fingers. Of course, Deni didn't notice until she sat down for dinner at Enzo's (or rather, the waiter noticed). Yuck.

Yes, your own shirts can work

Cherie was determined to wear her own shirts. She liked wearing them better than her husband's because he's proportionately much bigger than she is and she felt that she looked messy in his. She preferred her shirts more fitted. A few of the shirts she previously owned worked well. They were women's shirts (classically styled, either solid or striped) and were on the boxier side. The difference was that the shoulders, sleeves,

To make your husband's shirt yours, try:

• Rolling or folding up the sleeves to a length that's comfortable for you.

• Wearing a white T-shirt underneath to make it more feminine.

• Wrapping a scarf around your neck. This works with the classic feel of the men's shirt.

• Wearing a sweater tied around your waist (to give some dimension to the shirt and to sort of rein it in). You will probably be able to do this only in your earlier months. If you don't feel comfortable at the thought of this, definitely don't do it. To look chic, you need to feel comfortable and have full self-confidence in it. If the sweater is fine gauge (a thin sweater), it will tie nicely. Don't try it with a heavy sweater. You shouldn't do that even if you're not pregnant . . . it's way too bulky.

and chest all fit just a little more tailored. She felt more like herself in these than in any other type of shirt.

Sweaters

It goes without saying that those favorite tunic sweaters you've been wearing all along will work as your belly looms larger and larger. You and only you will know when they're getting too snug.

Body-hugging tops

Sometimes it's fun to wear a top that's clearly not meant for maternity and that really shows your belly. Why not? As long as you feel good about your body and you're confident, go for it. Our friend Libby loved wearing her Gap ribbed turtleneck sweater, which hugged her belly tightly. She'd toss on a blazer, but leave it unbuttoned so you could really see her belly. It's fun. How often do you have a baby actually bulging from your belly? Once, twice, *maybe* three times in your life.

Now that you've selected your essential

pieces for the next nine months, how in the world are you going to make them work for the rest of your pregnancy? Here are some style tips:

A blazer

Your basic black tunic or your classic shirt will look great with a blazer. It's great for casual evenings out when you either need a jacket for warmth or want to look a little nicer. If you pair your black tunic and leggings with the blazer, the simple lines will create a slimming effect. It will give you a fluid line from the top of the tunic down to the bottom of your legs. Your blazer should be somewhat unconstructed (refer to Chapter 3, "Closet Shopping"). Anything that's designed to be form-fitting isn't going to work. Leave it open (you probably couldn't close it if you tried). Just check in the mirror to make sure the tunic and blazer are the same length. You definitely don't want your hem peeping out of your jacket. *That* is tacky.

Dinner at 8:00? Sometimes you want to look nice without being overly dressed. We have a method called the "scarf shirt" that will take you out at night and vastly expand your horizons if you're confident enough to try. We credit this to our friend Evelyn, who wore it nearly every time she went out. Here's how: Take a colorful medium-sized square silk scarf and sew on a piece of elastic from top left corner to top right corner. Then sew another one from bottom left corner to bottom right corner. But make sure the bottom elastic is big enough to stretch over your belly (if you find that it's not stretching enough, cut if off and sew in a bigger piece when you need it). Voilà—you've got a silk "shirt" in a beautiful pattern or color to wear underneath your blazers. Wear it like a tube top—remember those?

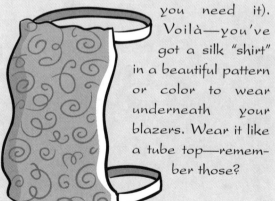

If you need to go to a dinner or want to look a little more dressed, try wearing a blazer without a shirt underneath—and show a little cleavage.

Vests and cardigans

If you have a vest or cardigan that's big enough, it will look great over your tunic. Unbutton them when they start to get tight. If you really love cardigans and want to continue to wear them throughout your pregnancy, you may need to purchase a new one if yours is either not long enough to cover your shirt or not wide enough to drape properly around your new, ever-blossoming belly. If this is the case, try going to a large-size store (or the large-size department of any department store) for the best selection. The reason we suggest a women's-style cardigan, rather than a big men's cardigan, is because women's cardigans have bottoms that are wider and less fitted than men's. They tend to fall straight down from the shoul-

ders, while men's, classically, have tighter ribbed bottoms that won't work with a tunic when your belly gets huge. Same goes for vests.

Jewelry

Keep it simple. One bracelet or a great pin may be enough. Pull up your treasures of years gone by and rediscover chokers, long necklaces, earrings that have been lying dormant on your shelves. You might just find the perfect bauble to give the outfit a little zing, making your basics appropriate for, say, a baby shower. Some pieces may look funny as you hold them up, but they just might work with your tunic and big new belly. You know the old saying: Try it, you just might like it!

Other accessories

Beyond jewelry, try toying with your footwear, bags, and scarves to give your dress a different look:

High boots with flat heels. This more funky look is great for daytime or a night out with friends. Just accessorize accordingly and make sure the hosiery you plan to wear will stretch over your belly.

Loafers. Try the high loafer that made its appearance on the fashion scene a few years ago and has since become a classic. It's an especially good choice to wear with a dress—comfortable with a bit of height—always important when wearing a dress. Flat loafers work, too, for a more relaxed look. Seven months pregnant with her first, Jody was spending a Saturday running around the city with some friends. She was wearing her long-sleeved Belly Basics dress with DKNY rubber-soled velvet boots that were so heavy on her feet that it really became an effort to walk. Her friend Bonnie noticed her plight and was obviously sympathetic, as she too had gone through a recent pregnancy. She insisted that Jody try a particular thick-soled rubber-bottom shoe from J. P. Tod's. At this point, Jody was willing to try anything, and the store, coincidentally, was around the corner. The shoe had the rubber bumps on the

bottom like a driving moccasin, but it had firm support from a thick, substantial rubber sole. It looked adorable with the dress (and leggings, too). Needless to say, Jody wore them out of the store and for the rest of her pregnancy and is still hooked on those shoes. The key to your footwear? Think beyond what you would normally wear on your feet with a dress. Be a little more daring and creative.

Different-colored shoes. If your dress is black, try wearing a different-colored shoe. By "different" we mean different than your dress. You might have some shoes in your closet than are a great fashion color—maybe something you bought on a whim. Try them on with the dress (or they may work better with leggings— try both and see). A black dress with shoes in, say, midnight blue, can be really fabulous. If you experiment with a fun color, keep your jewelry to a minimum. The shoes should be the main focus.

Work boots. Wear them with thick opaque hose and a beat-up leather jacket for a fun look (motorcycle jackets are great—naturally oversized for your pregnant belly, and a fashion perennial).

Colored or textured opaques. Don't just stick to black hosiery; have some fun with your legwear. Try a different hue or texture—preferably ribbed cotton. And remember that *color* doesn't necessarily mean *bright* color. Neutrals like oatmeal or charcoal can make you feel different, too. If you can't find great colors and texture in maternity tights (you probably won't), buy extra-large nonmaternity legwear and roll them under your belly. They'll work fine for this purpose.

Different handbag. How about a fun color or pattern or an exotic shape—maybe something that's been sitting on your shelf for years. It'll give your dress a lift.

Scarves. The key accessory. Even if you normally shudder at the thought of wearing a scarf, you should at least consider wearing one when you're pregnant—especially in your last trimester. We can't tell you how important they are to changing your day-to-day look—and to detracting attention from your belly! When you need to spark up your outfit for a quick dinner with your friends and don't feel like changing, just throw on a scarf. The epitome of "classic," they help dress up a pair of jeans for a day when you need to be just a bit more than just casual. In Chapter 3, we gave you different ideas on how to fold your scarves to achieve various looks. If you don't already own any scarves, there are lots of inexpensive ones that you can pick up in any discount store. Look for a pattern and color scheme that will go with most of your wardrobe. Don't be alarmed by big patterns or ones that you think just aren't you. When the scarf is folded properly and actually worn around your neck, you'll see very little of the pattern anyway. What you will see, and what's important, is the color. They'll fit no matter what, and furthermore, these scarves, like shoes and jewelry, are things you can have fun shopping for while *pregnant*. You can actually continue to wear them after the baby is born!

Your Key Casual Accessories

Jewelry
Bangle bracelets
Chain-link bracelet
Long silver necklace (slightly dressier and better for evening)
Funky beaded necklaces
Simple earrings

Belts
Leather belt with medium width (approximately 1") with a gold or silver buckle can have many uses while your belly is little
- try it over a cardigan
- use it to hold up your husband's jeans or shorts to achieve "paperbag waist" effect
- belt a loose tunic sweater

Shoes
Chunky boots: best with leggings or a simple dress
Loafers: an easy shoe that goes with all casual looks
Sneakers: best with no socks in the spring/summer when worn with a pair of leggings, or great with any type of shorts

Scarves
Medium square: looks great tied loosely around your neck or shoulders over a tunic or a sweater
Pocket square: tied neckerchief-style around the neck with a tunic or button-down shirt
Oblong: looks best with a solid tunic, sweater, or cardigan

casual
dressing

It's a tough job, but somebody's got to do it:
Work Clothes

Not so long ago, pregnant news anchors had to be shot from the waist up, sitting down behind their desk, for fear of exposing "the belly." If not, the station would receive piles of angry letters from the public, and the anchors risked losing their jobs. Being pregnant made them appear less serious on air. Times have changed. Today senators, supermodels, TV stars (remember Katie Couric's belly on the *Today* show?), and CEOs of major corporations have all been pregnant and proud of it. Check out *Seinfeld* reruns showing a very pregnant Julia Louis-Dreyfus. Her pregnancy was so accepted that her character, Elaine, wasn't even written in as pregnant. We all just quietly acknowledged it, and the show made only token efforts to hide it. Gone are the days of "retiring" at the first sign of a belly. It's not only acceptable to continue working, but expected. Anything you did before, you can do better pregnant.

But just between us, it ain't easy. Picture this: It's week eight, and morning sickness has reared its ugly head. You just finished puking in the trash can outside your office. You're white as a ghost, and you desperately need some ginger ale. But you look at your watch and it's 9:30 A.M. Damn. You stop in the ladies' room to wash your face, cup your hands under the faucet for a quick sip of water, and give your hair a quick brush. When you get to your desk there's a note from your boss: "You're late. Meeting started at 9:00 A.M. We're in the conference room." With pen and pad, you hustle over the meeting. Okay. Time to look like you're on top of the world.

Compared to combating the nausea, the heartburn, and the puffy fingers, getting dressed is easy. And the good news is that companies are more accepting than ever of flexible dressing. In past decades, women hid their growing bellies, camouflaging them from customers and clients. Now women dress to suit their growing bellies. While the thought of getting dressed for nine months of work probably seems daunting, there are a number of ways to make it more manageable. The whole process becomes simplified if you break it down and really focus on your individual needs. How strict is the dress code? How many important client meetings do you really have in a given week or month? What can you actually

If you love the idea of wearing trousers to work and can't picture yourself in anything else, try the homemade-panel route we described earlier. Pick up a maternity panel from a notions store for a couple of dollars and take it to a seamstress to have it sewn in (the instructions are right on the package). Your "new and improved" pants will work throughout your pregnancy, giving you the tailored-pant look you want for work.

get away with on a daily basis? At the beginning of Jody's first pregnancy, we were launching Belly Basics and her main concern was trying to look as professional as possible so that people—buyers, fabric companies, contractors, etc.—would take us "seriously." (A wardrobe in a box?! Sometimes we felt like Lucy and Ethel peddling some harebrained scheme). For days without meetings, her look could be more relaxed.

Okay, let's get down to business. Looking at the general picture, work environments fall into one of two categories—either a corporate environment with a strict dress code or one that's a little more relaxed and creative. If you work in the latter, you've got it made. The fashion ideas we discussed in Chapter 4 all apply to the work style you're probably looking to achieve. What we'll address here is for everyone else. It does take some strategizing to dress for the corporate world, so we'll go step by step. The key is to remember that you don't have to spend thousands of dollars to look great at the office. You need a few key items plus a knowledge of how to incorporate your existing accessories to change and modernize your basics. Your focus? To remain polished and professional. But don't underestimate the need to be comfortable. There's nothing worse than feeling like a stuffed pig when you're pregnant—you know, tight hosiery, high heels, and a fitted skirt. Ugh.

When your belly is still little

There are ways to make your current work wardrobe stretch—beyond the obvious ones like wearing your pants unbuttoned and unzipped. Here, we'll delve into some ways you may not have thought of. Remember, you're allowed to repeat your outfits. It's better to have a few great outfits than a whole lot of medicore ones.

To tide you over until you really have a belly to show for yourself, here are your two key items: 1) a short, black skirt, and 2) basic pants.

1. A short, slim, black maternity skirt

You can actually start wearing this right away, before your belly is noticeable to anyone but you. It'll be the perfect transitional item before you need to wear full-blown maternity clothes. Cotton/Lycra is one of our favorite fabrics for a skirt because it's the most comfortable for your belly while still looking appropriate for work. Consider gabardine or another heavier fabric if your company has a strict dress code and you'd feel funny wearing cotton/Lycra. Do keep in mind, however, that when it's worn with a jacket or big shirt, no one will notice the fabric content of your skirt. But your skirt will be the basis of your work wardrobe, so it should be something that you feel is appropriate. In addition, now's the time to dig out any elastic-waist skirts you may have uncovered while "closet shopping."

Our favorite waistband is the same as the one on our leggings: wide with no elastic to bind. Our favorite color for a skirt is, guess . . . black! We urge you to buy at least one in black. It's extraordinarily slimming and can easily be worn with many of your other clothes. And in a knit, the skirt becomes nondescript, which is just what you want. The last thing you want to

do when you're pregnant is draw attention to your middle, thighs, and bum. The skirt should be relatively short. We like to see a pair of legs peeking out from under a skirt hem—it seems to help balance the weight of a growing tummy. If you like long skirts—to your ankle—these can be great, too. We created a Belly Basics long slim skirt that we refer to as our "fifth" essential companion piece for The Pregnancy Survival Kit.

2. Basic pants

You have three options:

1) Inexpensive trousers. Think about buying some inexpensive trousers that are one or two sizes bigger than normal. Belt them until your belly fills them out. These will also be useful after the baby is born while you're working to get your shape back.

2) Pants with an elastic waistband. In certain fabrics like matte jersey or even wool blends, they're perfect for work. They'll fit you through most of your pregnancy. Cover your waist with a blazer, a simple tunic sweater, or even a big turtleneck. You should be able to get away with this for a while, certainly for the month or so when your belly has begun making its debut but you haven't shared the big news with your office.

3) Use the ponytail-elastic trick described on page 53 as a way to extend the life of your pants. The trick does not work if there isn't an actual buttonhole to thread through. If your pants or skirt have only a zipper and a snap, a hook and eye, etc., you'll be out of luck. They'll be harder to fudge. You can always use a safety pin, but, speaking from experience, that's not comfortable at all (just remember Cherie's mortifying safety-pin experience when she was pregnant).

Style tips

Work with these basic pieces the following ways:
Regular work blouses. If they're the type that is meant to be left untucked, you've got it made. If not, toss a blazer on over it and make sure it stays buttoned. Jody's neighbor Orlie, a bond rater on Wall Street, got away with this until the start of her sixth month. She didn't even announce her pregnancy to her office until she was into her fifth month. She rode the train to work each morning with Jody, who couldn't even tell she was pregnant (although Jody did secretly recognize the black Belly Basics skirt).

Fitted jackets. Wear your favorite fitted jackets, the kind you would normally button. As you progress (and after you have spilled the beans to your office) simply unbutton the bottom two buttons to give your belly some extra room. Keep unbuttoning as you need to (but wear a T-shirt underneath). We love this look. It softly accentuates your growing belly without really drawing attention to it. One of our buyers showed up for her market appointment like this, and the whole time we were busy making eye contact with each other, we were wondering, was she pregnant or had she just been munching too many late-night pizzas? Finally, after placing her store's spring order, she added a special order for a pregnant customer carrying twins—guess who?

A sleek sweater. A good look, maybe for a day when you don't have an important meeting scheduled. To look right it must be a thin, fine-gauge sweater—perhaps silk or fine cotton. Never a big bulky cable sweater. It should be loose and have a wide bottom like a tunic (refresh your memory in Chapter 3, "Closet Shopping") If you don't own one, think about picking up an inexpensive one at a discount store. Try belting it with a thin belt for a jacket look; wear a collared shirt underneath for a more businesslike look; or wear it loose and place your focus on your accessories. A scarf tied around your shoulders or some long pearls will be invaluable to you.

Basic "work" dress. We all have a "work" dress that we toss on when we don't know what else to wear. If it's loose fitting, it should easily cover your expanding belly. Even if it's fitted, it could still work: wear a blazer over it. It can be the perfect transition item until you're ready for your real maternity duds.

When your belly pops

Our friend Andrea, a publisher of a top fashion magazine, told us how she woke one morning in her eighth month feeling horrible. She dressed herself in baggy old pants and a sweater she usually wore only around the house. Her clothing choice matched her mood . . . miserable. When she arrived at work, she learned that there was a major press event that she was expected to attend. She had just enough time to grab her things and hop into a cab. She started to feel better, but when she got there, removed her coat, and looked down at what she was wearing, she was horrified. Surrounded by the most fashionable Manhattan editors, she suddenly felt very pregnant and very ill all over again. She sat in the back and slipped out before it was over.

No two ways about it, you'll have to wear clothes specifically designed to house your big belly. You need to look a certain way—pregnant or not. For women who work in corporate environments, pregnancy means making a small monetary investment in some good-fitting maternity clothes.

It can be daunting entering a maternity store. You're immediately tackled by a saleswoman eager to have you buy an entirely new wardrobe from head to toe. You've got to narrow your focus and zero in on your essentials. It's all about premeditated buys—whatever you do, don't get caught up in impulse buys. Here are the six key items to spend your money on (number 7 is the black skirt you've probably been wearing for months):

1. A black, long-sleeved tunic

This will probably end up being the single most important piece to buy for your work wardrobe. There are two secrets: Make sure it's the same fabric as your skirt so that they can be worn together, and make sure the styling and cut is simple enough to make it "forgettable." Long sleeves are essential even in the summer or in warm climates because they look infinitely more professional than short. Wear the tunic with trousers and skirts.

2. A white or neutral-color blouse

Even if you wear this blouse on Tuesday with the same black skirt that you wore with your black tunic on Monday, the outfits will look completely different—and that is the key to getting through until delivery day. A shirt that's already hanging in your closet could work. It just must to be long enough to look like it is meant to be worn untucked, and not like you forgot to tuck it in. It also has to cover your belly without straining. Or try your husband's shirt. If you work in an ultraconservative office, this might not work. But our accountant Debra (who is six months pregnant) pulled it off beautifully. Usually ultraconservative, she showed up looking chic in an outfit that for her was a little different. She had on black wide-leg pants, a white men's shirt, and a soft taupe blazer. She chuckled when we complimented her. Turns out she and her husband spent a late night at her parents' house and rather than drive home, they slept over and came directly to work. She raided her parents' closet before work and came out with her mom's pants (size 12; Debra's an 8) and her dad's shirt. The blazer was the same one she wore the night before. It worked. And it was a welcome change from her staid work wardrobe.

If you turned up empty-handed from your "closet-shopping" episode, either buy a basic blouse cut for maternity or, if you can't find a style you like, hit the large-size department (sometimes called Women's or something euphemistic like that). If the blouse feels too big all over in your current state, rein in the fabric with a safety pin in the back (a favorite fashion editor trick)—just remember to keep your blazer on.

3. A black blazer/cardigan

Some women, if they are petite enough, can continue to wear their regular blazers to work throughout their nine months. But most cannot. Look for one great maternity blazer with a one- or two-button closure, the most versatile and the best shape for your belly (you can try the large-size department if you prefer the styling or quality—large size has recently become a viable category for stylish good-quality clothes).

During Cherie's first pregnancy, she directed special events for a women's retailer. Her responsibilities included organizing designer collection openings, fashion shows, and even art exhibitions for the store. In this environment, you can bet she needed to look pulled together and current, which is not an easy task when you're pregnant. What Cherie used to do (remember, this was in the dark ages, before our invention of The Pregnancy Survival Kit) was wear one solid color of clothes from head to toe—often a full-length unitard—and then layer a blazer (usually dark muted colors, e.g., black, charcoal, cranberry, chocolate brown) over it. She accessorized it with a scarf and a pair of loafers. This look accentuated her "positives," which were her legs (in proportion to the rest of her growing body they appeared thin) and her collarbones (a unitard has a low, feminine neckline). The square

Check out the blazers by Emanuel, which are available at most department stores. They're designed for bigger frames, and they have a number of styles that work well for pregnancy. One style has a tie-front closure across the chest; it looks great with a bulging belly. Others are styled more like jackets.

shoulders of a blazer paired with a round feminine neckline also helps give the illusion of a longer neck, which makes a pregnant woman appear thinner and taller by detracting attention from her belly.

Or, if you prefer it, select something that's more of a cardigan. The difference is the fabric. A cardigan could be in a matte jersey or similar drapey fabric, while a blazer would most certainly be made of a fabric like a wool gabardine, silk blend, or even a linen blend if it's hot. When you wear your blazer or cardigan over a tunic, just look in the mirror to make sure they are the same length. If not, your tunic will hang out from underneath your jacket like a stray seat-belt strap hanging out of a car door. But when the proportions are right, you're there. Refer to Chapter 3 for a rundown of which blazer styles work best with a belly.

4. One basic vest

Picture a blazer with the arms cut off—that's the look you're going for. Again, it doesn't have to be a maternity vest if you can find an appropriate oversized one. A vest is often more comfortable than a blazer because your arms are free and unconstrained. For Lois, a woman who works in the Belly Basics department of Bloomingdale's, her "uniform" was a tweed vest over a simple black tunic and skirt. She picked up the vest in the ready-to-wear department a few years earlier. *Note:* While this is an excellent addition to your work wardrobe, if you have to cut back on something, this is the one essential we'll allow you to skip (but only if you really have to).

5. One basic pant suit

(Or skirt if you can't wear pants—but this is the nineties, isn't it?) You have two main choices here. Either buy the simplest, most basic maternity suit you can find, or go for "The Big Suit." Remember Diane Keaton in *Annie Hall*? That's the other option here—buy an inexpensive suit in a big size from a designer or manufacturer that you feel comfortable wearing. If you normally wear a size 6, a 10 or 12 will probably work. If you are above a size 6 or 8 to begin with, stick to maternity clothes—this option is not for you. The look is pure Annie Hall with droopy shoulders and baggy pants. For some people this is a better option than trying to find

Something to keep in mind when you look for tailored maternity pieces: Oftentimes the fabric doesn't have enough give to it, and your belly will have a hard time squeezing into it at the end. Our friend Lauren, a stockbroker in Boca Raton, had to cut open the waistband of her maternity suits so often toward the end that her husband, Michael, began carrying around a pen knife with him. Don't blindly trust the salespeople, who'll be quick to assure you that it'll go the extra mile. Stretch the fabric with your own hands to make sure it will.

an acceptable maternity suit of equal quality. Where can you find a suit like this? Check out sale racks and upscale discounters like Loehmann's. Our friend Yvonne, who at the time was the designer clothing buyer at a fashionable chain store and is normally a size 8, bought a size 14 Donna Karan camel suit off the sale rack at Saks. She wore it through her whole pregnancy and continues to wear the jacket once in a while over big sweaters. *Note:* Whichever option you choose, utilize both the blazer and the pants/skirt from your suit as separates, too, to extend your fashion options even further. By the way, if you think you can get away with it, you can use the blazer from your suit as your one and only. This is a great money-saving idea if you don't need to wear a blazer every single day.

6. A basic black dress

The world's simplest "outfit." When you have a dress that's basic and monochromatic—again, black is the most versatile and most slimming

color—you can wear it several times a week, and no one will even notice that it's the same dress. Depending on how progressive your company's dress code is, you may be able to get away with cotton/Lycra. Do keep in mind that no matter how strict the code, it relaxes a bit when you're pregnant. You can try testing the limits. Our friend Sarah, a lawyer on Wall Street, didn't think she'd be able to wear our Belly Basics cotton/Lycra dress to work. We encouraged her to try. Well, what do you know, her company had no problem with it (she even got a compliment from one of the partners); in fact, she set a standard for other pregnant associates. If you already know that you simply won't be able to get away with it (bummer for you—your dry-cleaning bills are going to be sky high), look for a dress in a wool or rayon-blend fabric.

Accessories

Once you're comfortable with your dress and have started wearing it to death, you'll need some tips on how to make it look new and exciting from day to day. Our friend Elyce, a fashion editor at *Women's Wear Daily* (the fashion trade publication), looked fabulous during both her pregnancies. When asked what she attributed her pregnancy style to, she could only recall one dress, which she wore at least once a week, changing the accessories every time she put it on. It was a swing dress in a soft, muted color. She felt extremely feminine in it, and she must have exuded that confidence; each time she wore it she received a barrage of compliments. But her secret weapon was her accessories. At the time, big, bold accessories were the rage. She used to layer strands of beaded necklaces on top of one another and pile on big bracelets. These days accessories are small and very personal but equally important (with the way fashion changes, the pendulum can swing back at any moment). The right accessories make a dress.

A common side effect of pregnancy is swollen fingers—sometimes painfully so. They may become so enlarged that you'll be unable to wear even your wedding band. Thankfully this doesn't happen to everyone (Cherie escaped both times, and Jody suffered only once). One way to continue to "wear" your rings is to put them on a secure (and we do stress the word secure) chain around your neck. It'll look like a charm necklace—very chic. Just be extra careful to remember where you put it when you take it off to sleep.

An easy way to choose accessories is to lay the dress on your bed or floor as you are getting dressed and throw a few different accessory choices onto the dress—earrings, maybe a necklace or scarf, a bag, and a shoe. It's easier to see everything this way, and you don't feel as committed to your choices as you would if you spent five crucial morning-minutes struggling with a clasp. Be wary of a long necklace though—it won't hang right over your belly. Stick to chokers or necklaces that come just a few inches below your collarbones.

Stock up on your maternity hosiery. When you're sitting at your desk trying to get some work done, the last thing you need is to have your hosiery digging uncomfortably into your belly. Look for hosiery with a wide band that will rest comfortably on your tummy. Pick one you like and buy dozens. We were in one of our stores when a woman, briefcase in hand, came running into the department waving her Visa card. "Give me a dozen sheer and a dozen opaque black. Charge and send."

Style tips

How to camouflage the fact that your dress shows up at work almost as often as some of your coworkers?

• Belt it to show off any semblance of a waist you still have. This works only if there is no baby-doll seam under your chest or any other horizontal seam anywhere on the body of the dress.

• Wear a crisp, white, collared shirt underneath the dress and let the collar stick out if the dress's neckline is round or V-neck. The shirt needn't be maternity. Any white shirt that will close (even partially) over your belly is fine. You're using the shirt for the collar and only the collar.

• Experiment with different blazers over the dress. If the blazer is full and long, say to your fingertips, this will make the dress look totally different—how could it not? You're practically covering the whole thing up. Jacket-style blazers look especially good.

• Tie a classic-style scarf (think Hermès) around your shoulders (see page 28 for scarf tips). Make sure you show a lot of scarf. It adds color and pattern to your dress, and draws attention away from your tummy.

• Try pins (even if they make you feel like your mother), pearls, gold necklaces, or silver chains (look again at the jewelry section starting on page 25 for more ideas). If you normally don't wear jewelry at all, try it at least once. If you really feel like *someone else,* leave the jewelry at home; you can live without it.

• Play up a different feeling each day. If on Monday you wear a colorful scarf, wear the same dress on Wednesday with a blazer and a choker necklace. Our friend Andrea, a handbag buyer for a chain of clothing stores, wore her black dress at least two to three times a week—and not a person noticed (although her husband got a little sick of it). She'd alternate her gold pendant necklace, her equestrian-print scarf, a navy gabardine vest, and, at least once a week, no accessories at all. As a matter of fact, once it even created a bit of controversy with her boss. She'd been wearing a colorful scarf draped over her dress all day; right before a business dinner that evening she removed it,

adding pearls instead. Her boss, who met her at the restaurant, was annoyed because he thought she had left work early to go home to change. Men! So unobservant.

• Try different opaque tights—black, textured, or a contrasting color instead of your usual run-of-the-mill sheer Lycra hosiery.

• Wear a cardigan rather than a blazer, especially for days without important business meetings (we both preferred it). It gives a blazer effect without constricting your arms. If you don't have a great one already in your possession (perish the thought . . . how could you have made it this far without one?), think about buying one.

• Reread the above style tips, thinking of your tunic—nearly all apply equally to a basic black tunic.

Summer style tips

• In hot weather, a dress is a natural (look for short-sleeved, sleeveless, or, if you work in an overly air-conditioned office, long-sleeved dresses). Think about buying a neutral-color dress in addition to the black dress you'll prob-

In buying a nonmaternity dress, keep the following points in mind:

• Don't buy something without trying it on. And when you do try it on, try rolling a sweater, or the nearest available bulky item, into a ball and shoving it under the dress. It's worth a good laugh and will help you judge whether the dress is appropriate to take you far into your pregnancy.

• Stay away from pleats on dresses as well as pants. They are generally not very flattering with a tummy, let alone a bulging pregnant one. Small accordion pleats, however, are a great look for a really skinny person.

• Remember that, as your belly gets bigger, the front of the dress becomes shorter than the back. The dress will actually hike up in front—this really only starts to happen at the bitter end. One suggestion is to take it to a tailor and have it lengthened in front about a quarter inch, while leaving the back untouched. If the dress is long (to your ankles), the hem problem will not be as apparent.

ably buy (if you haven't already). It stretches your options and looks completely different from black. If you can get by without wearing hosiery, you're really set. Otherwise, stick to sheers.

• If you go with bare legs, make sure your shoes are comfortable. Sometimes what starts out comfortable at 7:30 A.M. is wickedly painful by 5:00 P.M. Our friend Annie, a veterinarian in New York City, actually ended up taking her shoes off altogether for her last few blocks home. Can you imagine? With a week of near 100-degree temperatures, her bare feet swelled up like two hot dogs on a grill. She needed a good pedicure after that episode.

• White pearls are a classic look in the summer. Scarves are hot on the neck (and no one wants a sweaty neck), so you'll probably wear a lot of necklaces. Pick up imitation pearls for next to nothing at a flea market or an inexpensive chain jewelry store like Claire's. You can wear them long or short, single- or double-stranded, and they always look professional.

• Buy an inexpensive Japanese paper fan and keep it in your handbag. Jody was never without hers. She got it in New Orleans when she was seven months pregnant and was out listening to music with a friend who was five months pregnant. They were visibly hot. A woman sat down next to them and began to chat. Native born, she was an expert on dealing with heat. She reached into her bag and pulled out two pretty fans, handing one to each of them. It was a lifesaver. We can't tell you how many times she pulled it out to fan herself during unairconditoned cab rides or elevator rides up to meetings. You'll feel a little bit like a geisha girl at first, but you'll get past it.

The perception of pregnant women in the workplace has come a long way. Once you've made your decisions about how you'll present yourself for the next nine months, you can certainly appreciate what our mothers and grandmothers went through hiding their bellies behind layers of unflattering clothes. Women

have come too far for that nonsense. Let's play up our bellies and have fun with our style—and let's get down to business.

Addendum: business trips

"How can you send me away when I'm pregnant?" It does seem a little unfair. You feel like you should be exempt. But, pity, your boss will

If you are 5'0" or under, buy a basic tunic and wear it as a dress. There is not much difference in styling, but there are big differences in price. A few years ago we had a product called "Two Tops in a Box." It was just that—two different colored tunics packaged together. Throughout the season we noticed tremendously high sell-throughs in our size smalls. Turns out short customers were snapping them up as dresses. Smart!

not see it this way. He or she will continue to think of you as a regular person who's able to go wherever they need you to go (until, of course, the middle of the last trimester—at that point you ain't going anywhere). We both traveled extensively during our pregnancies. In our field, a big belly wasn't going to get in the way; on the contrary, it was always a topic of conversation (people used to insist Jody's belly must be a fake!).

Once you've resigned yourself to the fact that you will be going (probably more than once), focus on how to make it easy for yourself. The philosophy behind Belly Basics—core pieces that are extremely versatile—makes travel exceptionally easy. Your work wardrobe is probably already whittled down to necessities—one favorite in each "category": skirt, blazer, shirt, tunic, etc. Add a pair of leggings—for the plane ride and for after-work hours—and some key accessories, and you'll be as prepared as any good Boy Scout ever could be. Keep in mind:

• Plan on wearing skirts, tunics, blazers, and leggings more than once.

• Wear a little T-shirt underneath your tunic and dress—pack a few—to keep feeling fresh.

• If anything spills, spot clean it with soap and water (another reason black clothes are great).

• Pack things that won't wrinkle. When you expect to wear the same pieces two or three times, wrinkles just don't fit into the plan.

Case study: Last April, Jody traveled to Nordstrom in Oregon while six months pregnant. Her plans during her trip were quite diverse, including:

• Speaking at a "mothers-to-be" seminar for fifty women

• Meeting with store executives

• Appearing on a morning TV talk show

• Flying a total of nearly twelve hours

She packed her five key pieces: black tunic, slim black skirt, black dress, blazer, and black leggings. She added a few key accessories and was ready for anything. Here's how she did it:

• On the plane: leggings and tunic

• Business meetings: slim skirt, tunic, and an Hermès scarf

• The fashion seminar: dress with scarf

- TV appearance: slim skirt, tunic, and blazer

  When an event popped up that she hadn't planned for—dinner with her buyer—she was prepared: She wore the dress, this time with a silver necklace. Five basic pieces were able to do everything.

Your Key Work Accessories

Jewelry

Short pearls

Pendant necklaces

Button earrings—preferably pearl, gold, or silver balls

Pins of all shapes

Shoes

Stacked-heel loafers for skirts and dresses

Low loafers or pumps for slacks

Scarves

Big square scarf open over shoulders

Big square scarf fastened with a scarf ring

Small pocket square in blazer pocket

Don't sweat it:

Activewear

"A quick game of tennis? Sure, I'd love to. See you in a few." You hang up the phone and grab your racquet and balls, picking up your tennis shoes on the way. As you head for your bedroom to change, it dawns on you. "Tennis clothes . . . tennis undies. What in the world am I going to wear?" No matter how much planning goes into your seven-day-a-week wardrobe, it's going to the beach, playing an easy game of tennis, or even taking a brisk walk with your girlfriends that may end up throwing you for a loop. With this chapter as a guide, you'll be prepared for any situation you might face, barring any unforeseen urge to go bungee jumping.

Swimwear? Yikes!

You made plans to go to the beach with some friends next weekend, and now you realize that you're expected to show up in a bathing suit. Ah, a fate worse than death to a pregnant woman. You didn't think about the potential crisis you were creating when you casually made the plans. While this pattern of thought is common, it's totally backward. Your belly is absolutely beautiful, and so is the rest of your body. Everyone feels fat when pregnant—even those women who look like they're carrying little basketballs in their tummies. But to the rest of the world, they just look pregnant, period. Believe us, no one is ever going to look at you and think, "Boy, is she a fat pig." What they will think is, Wow. How amazing. She's got a baby growing inside of her. So don't try to hide it. If you do, you'll be the one to suffer—like our friend Danielle, who showed up at the beach seven months pregnant, in baggy blue shorts and a big University of Wisconsin T-shirt. We assumed the T-shirt and shorts would eventually come off like ours did, but they never

A word about zippers, ruffles, and bows: They don't belong on a pregnant woman's body. Ever. Especially on a bathing suit. Simplicity is best. The "bells and whistles" will attract undue attention to your swimsuit and your figure. We've all seen some doozies. (Our favorite? Cherie spotted it in South Beach. It was a floral suit with three rows of pink nylon ruffles running across a pregnant woman's rear.)

did. It was nearly 95 degrees and Danielle couldn't take a dip because she refused to put on a swimsuit. She was miserable. Granted, we've all felt like Danielle at some point, but what you've got to keep in mind is this: Forget about what you *think* everyone else will think. You've got a baby growing inside of you. Give in to your body and let yourself feel good. Recently we had a Belly Basics photo shoot for our spring collection. Our model was literally about to give birth (seven days later, she did);

she looked fabulous and was a real trooper when we photographed her in our new black swimsuit. She came out of the dressing room in front of eight men and six women without a second thought. All eyes were on her because pregnancy is such a miracle that it was incredible to see "it" covered only by a thin swimsuit (especially for men, we think, who can't even fathom what it must feel like). What to wear? Our motto: Less is more, and the simpler the better.

Certainly in your first trimester, and probably in your second, you can get by with a regular swimsuit. Here's how:

Size. Buy a suit at least a few sizes larger than your usual size.

Stretch. Buy a suit with a minimum of 10 percent Lycra or spandex to give you optimal stretch. Pull the fabric with your hands to test how much it's going to give. Don't feel funny buying a 14 if you normally wear an 8. Believe us, it's much better too big than too small. You'll know when it's time to switch to maternity because your suit will start to hike up on your upper thigh, exposing more than a little skin in the process.

Jody found that out the hard way during her first pregnancy. She was into swimming laps (great for the baby!), and during her first trimester she bought a new suit, one size larger. Three months later, she could barely squeeze into it. The swimsuit was a Speedo, meant for serious swimming, not serious stretching.

Style. Buy simple styles in solid colors—they're the most slimming.

When it's time to switch to maternity

We know, the swimsuits can be hideous. But if you adhere to some simple pointers, you'll be no worse for the wear. Here's a rundown of the different styles available:

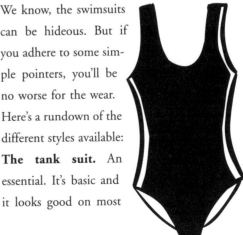

The tank suit. An essential. It's basic and it looks good on most women. A tank suit deemphasizes your chest and seems to cover up any upper-body bumps and bulges. It's best in a solid color, preferably a dark one (always the most slimming). This is our favorite type of one-piece because it is simple and it gives you just enough coverage, without calling attention to any specific part of your body.

We feel so strongly about this style, we felt compelled to design our own. Ours is a basic black tank suit in cotton/Lycra. Very cool. It grows with you. The swimsuit is cleverly constructed so that there is extra stretch around the belly for when your belly has a growth spurt, but to the casual viewer there is nothing out of the ordinary.

The "pouch" suit. This has that extra bit of material that forms a kangaroo-like pouch for your belly. Though not the most beautiful suit, it's flattering for women carrying all around their middle (pear-shaped). The pouch is loose and hides *all* your bumps and bulges. Some women love this type of suit and wouldn't dream of wearing anything else, like our friend Julie, who wore the same navy "pouch" suit every weekend the entire summer. Were we happy when Sam was born in mid-August! *Note:* If you're carrying small or are petite, this is not the suit for you. It will make you look dumpy—like you're parading around in a big plastic bag.

The V-neck suit or wrap suit. This lengthens your upper body by creating an **X** that starts at the top of your shoulders and continues down to your upper thighs. It's a very feminine suit and is very flattering on women who consider themselves short-waisted. It also helps detract attention away from your "bull's-eye" belly, giving your newly acquired cleavage a little play. Look for a suit with simple lines and stitching, and try to stick with solids. Stay clear of stripes (especially horizontal) or patterns.

The empire-styled skirt suit. This swimsuit has a looser top piece layered over it that begins mid-torso and hangs down like a dress or skirt. This look can be quite slenderizing, deemphasizing your bulging middle. Empire-waisted suits are actually very chic. (Norma Kamali has a whole collection of them in nonmaternity—something to think about if you're planning on wearing a nonmaternity suit.)

The underwire or push-up one-piece suit. Great for smaller-busted women because they're usually cut pretty low and shallow. It's the perfect way to show off a little cleavage—it can be like Christmas all over again if you're small- to medium-sized. But if you have humongo boobs, they could actually fall out of these cups.

Bikinis

Everyone has an opinion about bikinis on pregnant women. Some say, "What?! I never wore a bikini before, I certainly wouldn't be caught dead in one now." Then there are women who have worn bikinis in the past but wouldn't dream of wearing one pregnant (like Cherie). And then there are die-hard bikini wearers—women who have worn bikinis their entire lives and would never dream of stopping. Jody is one of those people. When Grant was due last August, her belly was huge during prime beach weather. She wore bikinis, one size larger. She would have been miserable in a one-piece. When she was eight months pregnant, she spent a rainy weekend with some friends in the Hamptons. But on Sunday afternoon it finally cleared, and Jody put on her bikini and headed for the pool. It was amazing what happened. The two other couples at the house, neither of which had been pregnant, were mesmerized. The guys, who had barely commented on her pregnancy the whole weekend, all of a sudden were at her side asking all kinds of pregnancy questions.

The women too. One of them even asked to touch it! If you can deal with this type of inquisitiveness, then by all means, wear your bikini. Just remember to wear a lot of sunscreen. Ouch!

At the *very* end of your pregnancy, you'll probably be uncomfortable wearing a bikini (even Jody put hers away). Your belly may have started to drop or you may just be enormous by this point. Either buy an inexpensive one-piece suit in the largest size available, or borrow from a bigger friend (if you plan on doing a lot of beaching). But to tell you the truth, at the very, very end you might not feel like putting on a swimsuit at all.

Cover-ups

Once you've settled on the type of suit you're going to wear, you've got the battle half won. Now you need to focus on your cover-up. Sure, you can wear your husband's big T-shirt or a pair of elastic-waist shorts. But even if these items fit, they'll look a little too sloppy and

The cover-up should be similar in color to your bathing suit so that when you take it off, it won't be such a noticeable "unveiling." Picture this scene: You're wearing a black cover-up all morning at the pool; then in the early afternoon you get hot, take it off, and wham . . . there's your bright red swimsuit!

very unflattering. Cathy, an old college friend and a real character, threw us all for a loop. When she was seven months pregnant and putting on her bathing suit for a pool party, she couldn't help but laugh at her own reflection in the mirror. She was about to bag the suit and go the T-shirt-and-shorts route when a crazy scheme popped in her head. She ran downstairs to her dining room, grabbed the round floral tablecloth she had picked up for $3 at a yard sale, cut a hole in the middle of it, and popped it on over her head. Admiring her reflection in the mirror, she was satisfied. She looked sufficiently ridiculous and decided to wear it over her suit. Her mission was obviously to poke fun at herself, but on the contrary, we were both there and can honestly tell you, she was the hit of the party. Everyone laughed and no one cared about her bathing suit. In fact, when she took the "muumuu" off, we were shocked at how great she actually looked in her suit. We talk about it to this day!

Here are our more fashionable cover-up suggestions:

A sleeveless tank dress. If you have already found or can find a simple little tank dress, it'll be perfect as a beach cover-up. It gives you a bit more coverage than a shirt does in areas like your thighs and butt (where, god knows, we could all use it). It should probably be maternity so the proportions are right and the front doesn't start to hike up as your belly grows (nonmaternity dresses can work, too, if you are a smaller-framed person).

A little tank dress is great because it's loose fitting, and if you end up wearing it much of the afternoon it will help keep you cool. It's also extremely versatile. You can throw on a pair of pretty sandals and go straight out to lunch or dinner.

Your husband's button-front shirt. We love this as a beach cover-up even when you aren't pregnant, and when you are, it's that much better. Everyone has one in her closet . . . er, his closet (at this point, isn't it sort of the same thing?), and it looks great on all body types. Grab one of his lightweight shirts (the white

And here are the cover-up don'ts:
• A robe. A terry-cloth robe is fine to throw on after a swim when you're not pregnant, but when you are, it makes you look frumpy. All you need is a hair net and some Ponds cold cream for your face and the look would be complete!
• A T-shirt. A T-shirt over a bathing suit creates a no-win situation. If the shirt is too small, it'll hug your belly and expose your tushy and if it's too big, like an XXL, it's going to look sloppy.
• Gym shorts. Unless you've got a tiny little belly and extremely long, thin legs, forget about it.

ones are the best), even after he's "gently" worn it—you're only going to sweat a little more in it anyway. Roll up the sleeves, and either button it or leave it open. Try to pick an older shirt, or one he doesn't wear all the time. Cherie grabbed Daniel's favorite white shirt, which looked to her like all the rest, and cheerfully wore it to the beach. He didn't notice it until two hours later when they were sprawled out on the sand. Daniel wasn't thrilled, to say the least. Supposedly it was the only white shirt that didn't hug his neck the wrong way. Oops!

The sarong (AKA, the pareo). *What?* A sarong for a pregnant woman? Are we *nuts?* No way— it happens to look fabulous on women who carry small or all in front. Sarongs are so feminine. If you already own a few and love to wear them, just take one and wrap it around your belly. If it's the same color as your swimsuit, it

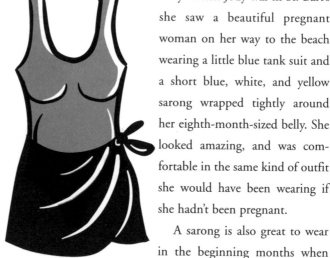

sarong over swimsuit

can be quite slenderizing, too (elongating your body). Wrap it as you normally would, but make sure to cover your whole belly. We love this look and think it is so chic over a pregnant belly. When Jody was in St. Bart's she saw a beautiful pregnant woman on her way to the beach wearing a little blue tank suit and a short blue, white, and yellow sarong wrapped tightly around her eighth-month-sized belly. She looked amazing, and was comfortable in the same kind of outfit she would have been wearing if she hadn't been pregnant.

A sarong is also great to wear in the beginning months when you want to cover your little "pouch." Cherie spent her first trimester in the summer heat, often with their friends at the beach. The sarong was her savior! Most of her friends didn't know she was pregnant (she didn't announce the news until her fourth month), and the sarong hid her bulge perfectly. She removed it only to swim (always leaving it within arm's reach).

A wrap skirt. This is a skirt that wraps around your whole body and ties. It's perfect during pregnancy because there is no defined waist—it grows with you. It may be a skirt that you already own, but keep in mind that if it is non-maternity, you will probably be able to wear it only during your first and second trimesters. It's a good option if you plan on going out after your day in the sun.

A sheer blouse. A sheer blouse worn over a bathing suit can be slenderizing and sexy (okay, now we've got your attention). Slenderizing because it's loose and drapey and hides "problem areas"—everybody has them—and sexy because you can still show a hint of skin. This look is especially good for women who carry extra weight toward the top part of their body, because it shows only an outline of your shape. The rest is left to the imagination. A black sheer blouse over a black bathing suit is definitely the slimmest look. When Cherie was in her seventh month, she and Daniel went to the Bahamas on a spur-of-the-moment trip. The day before they were leaving Cherie realized she didn't even have a bathing suit. Her mom happened to call during Cherie's packing frenzy and, in her typical motherly fashion, fixed everything. She rushed over that evening with her size-12 bathing suit (Cherie is a pre-pregnancy 6) and a sheer organza cover-up. It was perfect. The wrap bathing suit fit beautifully, and the sheer black cover-up was a lifesaver. Cherie wore it every time she went to the pool, making her less conspicuous (in her own mind at least) around all the skinny poolside women.

Workout clothes

The way we look at it is this: If you worked out before you were pregnant, don't even think of using this as an excuse to stop (unless, of course, your doc demands it). If you didn't work out before you were pregnant, you may want to power walk to stay in shape or take some easy prenatal exercise classes, which are designed specifically for this purpose. They also work on building the muscles you need to push the little one out. If you plan to keep your workout regime going during your nine pregnant months (really ten, but don't get us started on that) you must be totally prepared.

Being comfortable when you exercise is crucial. If you're not comfortable, you may be forced to cut your workout short. When our friend Olivia was pregnant, she was taking a class at Crunch, a Manhattan gym. She was wearing regular bike shorts hiked up over her fifth-month belly. Well, there just wasn't enough fabric to cover her belly without cutting her in the crotch. The more she pulled them to cover up her belly, the more they cut into her crotch, and the more annoying it became. She was forced to leave the class early—something no one wants to do after making the supreme effort to get there on time. Needless to say, she immediately called us to order a pair of Belly Basics bike shorts.

Here's what to wear when you're working out: First, ask yourself what you normally prefer to work out in. Only you know what works for you. It's a personal choice, perfected and refined over years of use. Try to stick to what you're most familiar with, amending it slightly as you grow. Here's the rundown:

Leggings/bike short and jog bra. Full-length leggings feel incredibly supportive, especially if you are suffering from varicose veins. They also give you a slender appearance, regardless of your shape. Bike shorts will always exaggerate your thighs but look great on women whose legs have remained slender. While you may have preferred bike shorts over leggings (or vice versa) before your pregnancy, you might switch temporarily.  Look for a cotton crotch either way. If your shorts or leggings don't have a cotton crotch, wear underwear with them (everything, and we mean *everything*, changes when you're pregnant—it's sort of like you spring a leak . . . get the picture?). Make sure they have at least 8 percent Lycra for support, as well as a comfortable waistband. The waistband is key because while you're struggling through forty minutes on a treadmill, you definitely don't want your waistband digging into your belly, nor do you want it falling down (which happened to Cherie after she cut the elastic on her leggings in desperation). There are a number of different types

Jog bras are great as a bra under your clothes, too. If your chest has gotten really big, you'll love the way it feels. It'll act as a minimizer, comfortably packing everything in—a far better option for some than an underwire. Our friend Maura wore a jog bra everyday under everything from suits to dresses to blouses—even her formal dress.

of waistbands out there, but again, it's a matter of personal preference. Before we designed our own perfect pair, we both bought normal bike shorts one size larger—they worked up to a point, and then became truly uncomfortable. Half of the time, Jody ended up folding the

waistband down under her belly to relieve the tension; Cherie, as you know, ended up slashing them, only to find they lost their elasticity after a few washes.

As for your jog bra, comfort is the name of the game. It should have excellent support and coverage. And while we're on the subject, let's talk about "back fat" (if you have it, you know what we're referring to; if you don't, be thankful and don't ask questions). In order to curtail "back fat" you need to make sure your jog bra is cut high under the arms. This holds it all in while giving you the support you need. Buy your jog bra at least one size larger. By its very nature, a jog bra is tight. You don't want to struggle putting it on each time you go to work out. And because it's tight, even if it *is* a few sizes too large, it will still give you the support you need. Toss on a T-shirt over it or, if you're brave enough, wear it alone and show off your belly in all its glory (but you've got to be plenty skinny or plenty confident to prance around the gym like that).

Unitard. A unitard—whether full length or bike-short length—looks great on a pregnant woman because it creates one consistent line from head to toe. You'll have to buy a new one—the one you already own won't fit as you get bigger. We suggest either buying one a few sizes larger or going with a maternity unitard. What you might not love about the former option is the loss of the tight fit that you're used to in a unitard. If you don't like the "bigness" all over, you can go with the latter, one designed for pregnancy. Look for a unitard with at least 8 percent spandex (for support), and don't forget about a cotton crotch! *Note:* A unitard can be a pregnant woman's worst enemy if she has a tiny bladder. Keep it in mind as you assess your options.

Gym shorts and jog bra. If this is your preferred workout gear, you're in luck because your husband probably owns a perfect pair of elastic-waist gym shorts just waiting to be plucked from his drawer. If not, and you have to buy a pair, make sure they're *jumbo*. It will be money well spent because you'll be able to give them to your

If you've already got a little one at home and can't imagine how you'll fit in a workout, try what Cherie did the second time around. She bought an inexpensive treadmill and exercised while Stephen played with toys beside her. By all means, try to keep your routine going. Not only will you feel better during your pregnancy, but you will have an easier time getting your shape back after the baby is born.

husband when you're finished. Gym shorts worn with a jog bra is of course harder to pull off the bigger you get. You can also wear gym shorts over your leggings for more coverage.

Body types

If you still aren't sure what to wear, here's a reference guide that will help you determine the workout gear that is best for your body type:

If you're all belly (like you swallowed a basketball): You can wear pretty much *anything* (and we all hate you!). An uncovered unitard would look fabulous on you, and since the rest of the pregnant population probably can't wear one, *you* should.

If you're carrying in all the "wrong" places (like you've got a tire around your hips): Go with black leggings or capri pants with a pair of gym shorts layered on top. Wear a unitard or jog bra—not a sloppy oversized T-shirt—to show off your upper body.

If you can give Dolly Parton a run for her money (and this is your main concern): Wear a great jog bra, covered by a T-shirt.

Underneath, wear leggings, a bike short, or a unitard.

If you're carrying *everywhere*, "head, shoulders, knees and toes, knees and toes": Black leggings and a big tee or long black tank will be your best option; they'll be the most camouflaging.

Golf

Over July 4th weekend, when Jody was pregnant with her first baby, she and David went up to Lake George. To her it seemed that everything they set out to do that weekend was taboo because of the pregnancy: Waterskiing. Sailing (the water was pretty rough). Even happy hour.

If you plan to work out during your pregnancy, do the same types of things you did before you were pregnant—don't introduce a new piece of equipment or a new sport. It's not fair to do to your body. By the same token, your body becomes conditioned to working out when you do it regularly, and eliminating exercise altogether would completely throw your body off. You just need to make it a little easier. Jody has always been a "step" fan and continued to be one throughout. She made it less difficult during the final month by taking one step away.

Everything, that is, except golf. It was then that they realized that golf was one of the best activities for them to do together. While they normally would play maybe nine holes on a given weekend, over this weekend they played eighteen each day. It was a great way to spend the afternoon—getting fresh air, exercising a tiny bit and being together. If you are already a golfer (or you always wanted to start), it's a great activity to do when you're pregnant. Because it doesn't involve great exertion, it's one of the few things that a pregnant woman can actually do without worry. We might also add that you should play as much as possible now, because once you have the baby, the opportunies to sneak away to play a quick nine holes will be few and far between.

Golf is a sport that has many etiquette rules, so golf attire is important. If you are playing at a country club or resort, you're going to have to follow their rules whether you're pregnant or not.

What you wear on top should be fairly easy: If your husband wears a big size, borrow one of his polo tops (if not, pick up an XL polo shirt).

Bottoms are trickier. Maximize your own shorts as long as possible with the rubber-band trick. Jody pushed the envelope so far that she ended up rubber-banding them together only when she was walking around the clubhouse; otherwise, when she was out on the course with just David, she would unzip her shorts entirely. You *will* reach a point when even this will no longer work. If your husband is considerably bigger than you, try wearing his shorts (if his are too small, go to Kmart and pick up a cheap pair of men's khaki shorts). With a big shirt on top, no one will notice that you're wearing men's golf shorts (check the maternity stores, too—you may luck out and find a decent pair of khaki shorts). Belt the waist with one of your own belts. If your own belts don't fit any longer, see if your husband has one of those woven leather belts without any buckle holes. They're perfect. If neither of you owns this kind of belt, you can pick one up inexpensively at the Gap—you'll definitely wear it post-baby.

When your belly gets really, really big, even men's shorts will no longer work. Try maternity bike shorts with one of your husband's XL collared shirts. You can rationalize that at least the shirt is regulation. Plus, by the time you're that big anyway, you become more of a conversation piece on the golf course. "You're *still* playing?" "Oh my, are you okay to play?" "You haven't had that baby yet?" You know, that sort of thing. When you look like you're a few days away from giving birth, people actually forget to take note of whether or not you're following course rules.

Tennis, anyone?

The same rules apply for tennis, a sport that you can continue to play when you're pregnant as long as you don't play too hard (doubles are a great idea as your tummy gets bigger). Cherie and Daniel play tennis whenever they get a chance, and thus continued to play during Cherie's pregnancy. The only thing that changed was the length of Cherie's tennis skirt—it inched up higher and higher each week. Cherie recalls, as if it were just yesterday, when Daniel pulled her off the court during a doubles match to tell her that more was showing than he cared for the world to see. After that memorable game, she went to the Gap and bought an inexpensive white polo dress (no waist), which suited her for another few months. If you have a basic T-shirt dress in white, it'll be perfect. Another option is to wear black bike shorts with a white A-line tank. These clothes (or something similar) are probably in your current maternity wardrobe. Especially toward the end, you should try to make do with things you already have. Stick with whites even if there are no "tennis whites" rules. Tennis is a mind game. If you look like a serious player, your opponents will most likely think you are one—regardless of how you're playing that day. But, no worry, being pregnant is always a good excuse for a bad game.

Hiking

This is a great activity when you're pregnant. Hiking is 80 percent walking, which is one of the best forms of exercise. You can hike with your husband or with your whole family (if you have older children), and it's the best way to see the scenery while on vacation. Dressing for a hike is fairly simple.

Supportive shoes are a must. The reasons are myriad: Your balance and coordination are a little off. The bigger you get, the more pronounced this becomes. Don't worry, it's nothing that will prevent you from doing what you want to do, but it is something to keep in mind. Supportive

shoes will protect your ankles from unexpected twists and will help you better grip the hiking surface, preventing bad falls. A sturdy shoe with gripping lug soles is the ticket. Try to wear an ankle-height boot because that gives you the extra support you need.

Bike shorts are the most comfortable when it's hot out. True, they may not seem like the proper hiking pant, but for a pregnant chick, they are. When you wear them with an oversized T-shirt, no one will notice the bike shorts anyway.

Be sure to bring along a big bottle of water, even if you are going on a short hike. You may think that since you're just taking a "walk" you don't need to carry water, but hiking or walking long distances (especially in the heat) is very taxing on your body. And by the way, have your husband lug the water bottle. You have enough to carry . . . don't you think?

Biking

First check it out with your doctor, and if it's okay, go for it. When Jody was in her third trimester last summer, she rode nearly every weekend with David and Jade, who loved to ride on the back of David's bike. If you're determined to continue riding your bike while pregnant, the main issues are sturdy shoes and comfortable bike shorts (hey, they ain't called bike shorts for nothing). Don't forget to wear a supportive jog bra, too. When you're pregnant, your boobs need much more support than before, to prevent them from bouncing this way and that. It also protects against post-baby sagging (not the most pleasant thought, but a reality for moms). Wear a helmet—something you should do anyway. David was fanatical about this with Jody. She definitely felt silly wearing a helmet as she casually biked through her neighborhood streets (her and all the six-year-old kids), but she did it anyway.

Biking can also be a great thing to do on a vacation. Cherie and Daniel did the California coast as a last hurrah before their first was born. Cherie was five months pregnant and feeling great during that brief period of bliss that seems to occur somewhere between the morning sickness early on and the complete exhaustion of your last few months. They packed a light picnic with tons of water and ended up riding twenty-five miles on mostly flat terrain—yes, they took many rests. It was certainly the most memorable day of the vacation.

When you're pregnant, it's sometimes hard to relieve tension and relax. No glass of wine with dinner. No uninterrupted sleep. Even an indulgent massage can be off limits. But physical activity is one way in which you can really let off some steam and make yourself feel good. You'll feel an energized boost, whether from a brisk walk around the block, a twenty-minute swim, a bike ride, or a friendly game of doubles. Get dressed and get moving!

Boo!

This is something you don't think about until October 25, when you realize you've been invited to a Halloween party and actually have to wear a costume. But, really, what does a pregnant babe dress as? Here are some ideas:

• A nun. People always get a kick out of seeing a pregnant nun. Cherie came dressed like this to Jody and David's Halloween bash two years ago—it was a big hit.

• The bull's-eye on an archery course. Wear a white top and white bottoms. Take colored tape—red, blue, yellow, and black—and lay it in concentric circles over your belly. Carry a bow and arrow to complete the effect.

• A snowman. Wear all white and sew three big black buttons down your belly. Wear a top hat and hold on to a carrot.

• A jack-o'-lantern. Wear an orange top and add two black felt triangles over your boobs for eyes, another one in the middle as the nose, and draw a zigzag mouth below it. Or, if you're daring, wear a cropped black T-shirt and black leggings (yes, your belly is supposed to be sticking out). Paint your belly orange and draw the jack-o'-lantern's eyes, nose, and mouth right on your skin (make sure the paint is nontoxic).

• A turtle. Feel like crawling under a shell? Turn yourself into a turtle by covering your belly with a big round piece of green felt. Use poster board to create two arms, legs, and a "head" to see out of.

• Cousin "Itt." Just slip on a ski cap and add a whole lot of light-colored yarn. Staple the yarn to the inside of the cap, making sure it comes down about five feet (almost to the floor). Make sure you cover up your face and put on a pair of sunglasses.

Put on your dancing shoes:
Formalwear

It can truly be exasperating trying to find something, anything, to wear to a formal event. You want something that's different. Something that will allow you to stand out from the sea of black usually found at dressy events. One of those magnificent dresses you've seen floating from the pages of the latest fashion magazines. Yet you don't want to spend a fortune. The whole thing isn't easy . . . and we're talking about when you're *not* pregnant. Trying to do all this when you *are* pregnant is a completely different ball of wax. Your focus is going to be on different things. Rather than being concerned about finding something that's truly extraordinary, something that's going to wow the room, your new focus is now going to be on something that simply fits. And on something that won't break the bank. Dressing up. Oh, the agony of it.

Here, we'll give you suggestions on how to make do and still look appropriate, plus how to look over the top when you need to. Even if you don't foresee an event for which you'll need to be formally dressed, you can bet that one will surely crop up. It inevitably does. Let's think about your options. Obviously, different formal affairs call for varied degrees of dress. Before you completely freak out and go on a rampage for a dress that doesn't exist even in the chicest French boutique, you should assess your needs and map out a strategy.

There are basically three types of dressy occasions: daytime events, cocktail parties, and formal or black-tie events.

Daytime event

What: A christening, an afternoon wedding, a bar mitzvah, or a luncheon.

Attire: Men wear sport coats. Women wear appropriate dresses or suits, though skirts or dressy pants can work, too.

They say clothes make the man. We say accessories make the outfit. If ever your accessories are absolutely crucial, this is it. Sometimes your accessories can carry the whole darn thing. Pearls, jewels (real or faux), and baubles of all sorts are what grabs the eye. Think of the black wool skirt or basic black top you may be wearing as only a backdrop, and each treasure will take on increased significance because there is less of it. A woman usually wears just a few choice nuggets when she dresses up. Look through your jewelry box. Call your mother. Ask your mother-in-law. Just don't overlook it: jewelry, evening bags, wraps, or even a jeweled hair accessory can really jazz you up (see page 130 for a recap).

Tips: This is one time when it's nice to wear muted colors or pastel hues (no, we haven't lost our minds or anything, it's just that a pale pink suit can look stunning for a daytime event). Granted, they can be tough to find.

Six months pregnant with number two, Cherie was invited to her cousin's wedding. The party was at noon at Panevino, a chic Italian eatery. She wore a neutral colored shift dress with a string of pearls and her silk slingback, mid-heeled pumps.

Cocktail party

What: An evening party in a person's home, a restaurant, a social hall, or a hotel. It could be a business function, a Christmas party, or a birthday celebration.

Attire: Men wear suits or dark sport coats. Women should have a hint of evening to their outfit.

Tips: A dress, pants, or even a unitard (as an underneath layering piece) is acceptable if you wear it in the right way. Velvet and silk are two fabrics that won't let you down. Just one simple piece in velvet or metallic (like a blouse) can work paired with a black basic (we'll explore this more later in the chapter). Stick to darker colors. Light or pastel colors are usually wrong for cocktail attire—especially when you're pregnant. A long straight skirt in a knit is great if you want to make more of a fashion statement. Try pairing it with a loose, dressy blouse in silk, metallic, or velvet. Jody was invited to David's office holiday party at the last minute—"Oops, I forgot," he said, "spouses *are* invited." She found a long black tube skirt at one of those supertrendy stores for teenagers (the type where the music is way too loud—whoa, did we actually *say* that?). She wore it with an oversized velvet blouse she'd bought at the beginning of her pregnancy. She buttoned only the top button of the shirt, and underneath she wore a black stretch tank top. The look was cool and sophisticated without being all dolled up. If you want to look a little sexier, go short.

Formal or black-tie event

What: A nighttime affair in a hotel, synagogue, catering hall, country club, or even a tent in someone's yard. Perhaps a wedding, a charity event, or a business function.

Attire: Men wear either a dark suit or a tuxedo and women must be in true formal dress.

Tips: Stick to dark, sophisticated colors. A dress is the easiest way to go—long and short are both acceptable. We love either an empire-waisted dress or a swing dress (see Chapter 3, "Closet Shopping") for formal shindigs. Both can be sexy. But remember to show a lot of leg.

Once you've zeroed in on the appropriate attire, you must give some thought to the image you want to project, just as if you weren't pregnant. For your old college buddy's wedding, where you'll see people you haven't seen in years, you want to look smashing. For your husband's office party, you might want to blend in by opting for something more conservative. Assess the following: Do you want to make a statement or would you rather blend in with the crowd? Do you want to look sexy or conservative? Are you trying to play down your pregnancy, or do you want to flaunt it?

Okay. Now that you've got a feeling of what sort of look you're going for, read through our creative dressing ideas. Don't assume that you have to head directly to the closest maternity store. You have lots of options, and, in the upcoming paragraphs, we'll go in depth on each one. They include:

- Finding something in your own closet that can work
- Dressing up basics you already own
- Borrowing from a friend or relative—either maternity or nonmaternity clothing
- Discovering vintage
- The last resort: Digging into your wallet and buying something new, shopping at maternity and nonmaternity stores

It might be right under your nose!

Look through your collection of dresses. Don't forget about the ones hidden in your closet somewhere. Dresses without waists are obviously the best. You really need to take out each dress separately and reexamine it. It's funny how you remember dresses slightly differently from the way they actually are. Our friend Natalie pulled out a short hunter green dress with black disc sequins on it and was shocked to see that it had an elastic waist underneath the blousy top. She laughingly wore it to her girlfriend's wedding. The dress was nearly fifteen years old, but she had never gotten rid of it because it was quite a find back then. You'll probably be very surprised at what you can unearth in your very own closet.

Cherie recalls a similar situation. A few years ago her close friend Kim asked her to be the matron of honor at her wedding. She wasn't pregnant at the time, so you'd think it would be easy finding a dress. No chance. As she's a bit of a perfectionist, she was determined to find the perfect dress. It turned into a major production (even Jody got drawn into the search). So instead of finding the one perfect dress, she found three. She brought them all home, planning to return the runners-up. Turned out, one couldn't be returned. It was a long black velvet dress with an empire waist.

Keep an open mind with colors—they can create a mood. Brights make you feel bold and adventurous; pastels are a bit more romantic; neutrals are more sophisticated and quieter.

123
formal-
wear

Daniel hated it. He thought it made her look pregnant! She nixed it for the wedding and relegated it to the back of her closet. One day, nearly three years later and six months pregnant with number two, she was looking for a dress to wear to a formal business function. She rediscovered it in her closet. It was stunning. Daniel didn't recall the dress and commended her on her great find.

Don't look just at dresses. Other items can work, too. Jody was invited to the June wedding of an elementary school chum of David's (talk about an old friend). Only five months pregnant, she discovered a pair of white silk drawstring pants hanging in her closet. *Yes!* Searching for something to pair them with, she unearthed a fabulous sheer white pleated vest in luxurious silk. An outfit was made. She borrowed a white sleeveless cotton bodysuit from her mother-in-law to prevent the vest from being indecently see-through. A piece

from here, a piece from there—this could be the recipe you're looking for.

Back to basics

Remember when actress Sharon Stone wore a black Gap T-shirt with a Valentino jacket to the 1996 Oscars? Basics can mix easily with dressier items. Even a simple cotton/Lycra dress can work for a cocktail party or wedding when paired with beautiful pearls, silk shoes, maybe a fabulous wrap and an "up" hairdo. Do you have a big, sheer blouse/jacket? If not, you might want to think about picking one up (check out the blouse or formal occasion section of a department store or off-price store). This is the type of piece you'll wear again as a jacket. You can usually find it during any season—sometimes even on sale. It's perfect to wear over a basic tunic and skirt, a dress, or the way Jody wore it, over a full-length unitard. Seven months into her first pregnancy, she was invited to an old friend's wedding. Held in a gorgeous loft overlooking downtown Manhattan, the party was elegant and very formal. Some old friends were going to be there, as well as some business associates. She had to look smashing. She bought a full-length black Wolford bodysuit made of a shiny, luxurious fabric that softly hugs the body (which she could definitely wear again—and has!), and she topped it with a sheer organza jacket that she had from another outfit. Leaving it open, she had enough coverage of her tush and thighs to look elegant, but was able to flash enough belly to show everyone her little bun in the oven.

A borrower or a lender be

Let's think about this two ways. The first: Borrow dressy maternity duds from friends who've been pregnant. The second (this one is a little more creative): Think about people—your mother, good friends, sisters-in-law—who are not the same size as you. People whom you never would have borrowed from before because they may be a few sizes bigger than you. You

need to tread lightly though. Think about it— "Oh, I'm seven months pregnant with an enormous belly. Can I borrow one of your dresses?" Don't offend anyone (women are *so* sensitive)— ask carefully. But don't ignore friends and relatives of the same size, too. Whether they've been pregnant or not, they might have something that'll work for you.

It's fun to try on clothes together—something you may not have done since college— but don't forget to arrived prepared if you are going to shop in someone else's closet. Treat it as if you were really going shopping for a formal dress. Here are some tips to remember:
• Put on a little lipstick and run a brush through your hair. If you look a mess before you even slip the dress on, you'll probably be unhappy with the way the dress looks.
• Bring a pair of sheer hose and evening shoes to try on with the dress.
• Go on a day when you are feeling good about yourself. You need to be feeling somewhat comfortable with your body or you'll come up empty-handed.

• Though you may be tempted to take the dress home to try it on there, don't. It's more helpful (and much more fun) to hear feedback. How many times have you thought something looked terrific in the mirror and later realized that you never looked worse?

• Look at the dress critically. Remember that your friend's size and or body shape may be different from yours, and the dress was bought for her. Look at the shoulders and the waistline. Do they hit you in the appropriate places? Is the style flattering on you? If it really doesn't work, don't settle. You'll be miserable all night. Let this be your backup if other efforts fail. Cherie was five months pregnant with her first baby when she called her friend Karen in desperation. She needed a dress to wear to a formal dinner dance. They hid out in Karen's bedroom and played "dress up" for over an hour. Some of Karen's favorites looked absolutely ludicrous on Cherie. They're approximately the same height and weight, but their body types are completely different. After an hour, they came out with a winner: a fabulous Jil

Sander empire-waist dress (nonmaternity), a velvet wrap, and even an awesome necklace and earrings to wear with it. Now that's our idea of bargain shopping.

They don't make 'em like they used to

If your mom is anything like ours, she hangs on to everything. Nothing ever gets thrown out, it just gets moved into another closet. Usually into a storage closet that ought to have a "Do Not Enter" sign with a skull and crossbones on the door. Go for it. You may love what you find. Cherie discovered her mom's old stash in the attic when she was five months pregnant and ambled up to sift through some of her own memorabilia. She saw the "old clothes" boxes and was intrigued. They were filled with dresses—totally retro and back in style. Some were pretty outrageous, like the orange and silver miniskirt and matching halter (go, Mom!). Cherie came across a sleeveless, bell-shaped vintage lace dress with cream faux fur trim applied to the hem. It was simply stunning.

Each season we go back to the drawing board to design a new evening dress to add to our line, and each season we come back to our classic. It works. It's a dress in stretch velvet with a very slight empire waist (we change the color each season). With a flattering round neckline and slim sleeves, it falls elegantly and gracefully over the belly, stopping just before the knee. The velvet has a wonderful sheen to it, and it's comfortable, comfortable, comfortable!

She ran downstairs and tried it on (her mom was certainly surprised to see it after twenty-odd years). Because of the trapeze shape, it was perfect for Cherie's little belly. She just *had* to wear it somewhere. As luck would have it, her college roommate's wedding was the following month. She was the hit of the party and all night she felt really special in her mom's dress.

An old find can be even better than a new one when you're pregnant because the fabric and workmanship in vintage clothing are usually superior to today's maternity clothes. If your own mom or someone you know isn't a saver, visit a vintage clothing shop. Fashion *always* repeats itself. You're bound to find something current. If you are lucky enough to find designer pieces, they are usually timeless and can be worn again and again. Some formal vintage styles to look for:

• Swing or trapeze dresses from the sixties
• Empire-waist dresses
• Velvet, fur-trimmed, or beaded wraps, capes, or scarves
• Sheer organza blouses or any overblouse or jacket
• Tunics with beading, sequins, or luxury trims
• Silk mandarin collar jackets with frog closures
• Over-the-top jewelry

If you happen on a great piece but not an entire outfit, augment it with a basic, just like we mentioned on page 124 under "Back to Basics." A red mandarin collar jacket, for example, looks great with a pair of black straight-leg maternity pants (our friend Renee wore this to a charity benefit at her country club—her Chinese-style silk jacket was a find from a local thrift shop). If you've got one great piece that is important enough to carry your whole look, minimize everything else.

Let's go shopping

If you have thoroughly exhausted all other routes and still nothing . . . it's time to hit the stores. You have two choices: a maternity store or the formal occasions department of your favorite store.

A maternity store

The selection here is not huge—either you'll see something you like or you won't; just don't be cajoled into selecting a dress solely on the fit. It should look good on you and you should feel good in it. Pay close attention to:

The fabric. Silks, velvets, and other lux fabrics are all very expensive, which causes many maternity manufacturers to use an inferior substitute to keep costs down. If you think you're buying silk, check the label to make sure it really is silk. Know what you're buying.

The shoulders and chest area. It should fit you well. In other words, don't buy something looking like a big ole potato sack. You need to show that you have some semblance of a shape left.

How about a one-night stand? A new industry has burgeoned in the last few years: rental dresses. Sounds weird, but why not? Men rent tuxes. In New York City, a mom was the first to come up with this ingenious idea. She opened up a store that carries a full selection of dressy dresses—both maternity and non; you wear it and return it. What a concept. You don't have to be "married" to the dress. Renting a dress runs about one-fifth of what it would cost to buy one, so it's a great option for women with champagne taste on a beer budget. Check your Yellow Pages to see if there is such a store near you.

The neckline. Try showing a little cleavage—you might as well flaunt it; god knows you've probably got it.

Detailing. Look at the detailing—the buttons, the beading, the seams. Check the quality. Is it what you're accustomed to? With a formal dress, detailing makes all the difference.

The fit. Don't compromise on the fit just because it's maternity and you think this might be the only dress left in America to fit your Rubenesque body. Watch for too much fabric in places where you don't need it, like under your arms, in your chest area, and even around your hips. We never understood why maternity clothes were so oversized everywhere! Wearing a muumuu certainly doesn't do much for your self-image.

Your favorite department store or boutique

You might find a dress that's the perfect style to accommodate your pregnant tummy just hanging in the racks of clothes for the rest of the world. When shopping keep in mind:

Fit. There must be enough extra fabric to fully accommodate you in the final months—otherwise you risk having it hug your belly like O.J.'s infamous glove.

Size. Chances are there will be a time lapse between when you purchase it and when you actually wear it—you'll do a lot of growing between now and then. Because you don't want to outgrow it before you get a chance to wear it, keep the price tags on and try on the dress a week before your event just to be on the safe side.

Style. If you select a size or two larger (or three or four), you might even find a straight sheath that could work, if you're daring enough to pull it off.

Where to look in a department store

Formal-occasion department.

The large-size department. The selection of dresses in the large-size department is usually not huge, but hey, you never know. The dress of your dreams might be waiting there for you.

Main-floor accessories for everything but the dress. Wear something simple, possibly something you already own, and go hog wild in the accessory department: new "dancing shoes," a feather boa, an exotic evening bag, or even rhinestones, pearls, and faux gemstones are the perfect pick-me-up for a tired black dress.

Whether you finally settle on something old, something new, something borrowed, or even something blue (midnight preferably), this is your time to shine. Photographers, other guests, even the waiters fuss over a pregnant woman. You'll probably be the only woman there with a thirty-pound gut, so play it up and make the clothes work for you. In a few short months you'll be back where you started—a regular gal trying to stand out in of a sea of monochromatic black.

Your Key Formal Accessories

Jewelry
  long pearls
  pearl chokers (or any type of choker)
  rhinestone earrings
  antique/vintage jewelry

Scarves/capes
  sheer oblongs in florals
  velvet oblongs
  boas
  velvet and other luxury fabric capes

Handbags
  silk bags in brights or black
  beaded bags
  small jeweled bags

Velvet hair accessories

Silk shoes
  (try Dyeables brand in a low-heeled pump)

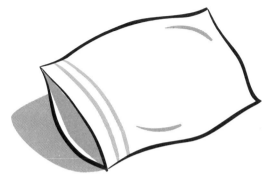

Slow down, you move too fast . . .
Bedrest

At the end of her second pregnancy, Cherie had a bout with strict bedrest. She looked at it positively—it was a wake-up call. She had been busy running around, working as hard as ever at Belly Basics and trying to give any leftover time to her son, Stephen, and . . . oh yeah, her husband, Daniel (somehow the husband gets the short end of the stick during times like this). Two months before her due date, without any warning, she went into preterm labor. In Florida during her Christmas vacation, of course. The doctors scared her right into bed when they looked her square in the eye and told her if she failed to follow their strict orders she could have this baby tomorrow. She quickly obeyed (they allowed her to fly home to New York and then that was it for her). She viewed this "sentence" as an opportunity to give her baby a peaceful time to grow before the big day. No more roller-coaster rides for baby as she ran out of the office at 6:02 to catch the 6:10 out of Penn Station. No more grabbing lunch in the car as she drove Stephen to his gym class, picking up two of his buddies on the way. She finally rested. Instead of giving birth at thirty-one weeks, when the whole ordeal began, Cherie gave birth at thirty-four weeks to a healthy baby boy, Jonathan.

We'll make no bones about it, bedrest is tough. While it might seem like lots of hot chocolate, bonbons, and fuzzy slippers, it's not. Nine times out of ten, bedrest means, quite literally, just that—resting in bed until you go into labor. Your bed (or couch) is now your office, your kitchen, your living room, and your bedroom. Make sure everything is easily accessible to you. After a day or so, you'll figure out exactly what you need. For Cherie it was a huge

pitcher of water, a few snacks (rice cakes, graham crackers, Goldfish—not very healthy, but yummy); the TV remote; a good book; lots of pillows (don't forget the one that goes under your legs); a pad and pencil; a telephone (absolutely crucial); and last but not least a small mirror and lipstick (always be prepared for unexpected guests). Keep your essentials within arm's reach. If you need more room and are forced to

Keep a jar of moisturizer next to your bed and remember to lubricate your skin, especially the skin that's stretching along your belly, thighs, and breasts. As if the stretching isn't bad enough, staying inside all day can be very drying to your skin.

replace your night table with an ugly card table, cover it with a tablecloth or something pretty.

Getting dressed while you're on bedrest should be a nonissue, one less thing for you to worry about. Hands down, comfort is most important. When you're lying on a couch all day, being uncomfortable in your clothes isn't even an option. However, as silly as this may sound, style is still important for many reasons. You do want to feel good about yourself—if you're wearing sweatpants and T-shirts every day, your self-image can't help but suffer. It's

> If you have an older child
> Remember to engage him—he'll need the extra attention. Have him join you on the bed and spend some quality time together. Play silly games like pretending the sheets on your bed are your secret hideaway tent (you know, like you used to do when you were little). Or just watch TV together, read stories, or color. Cherie had made one whole part of her bedroom a mini playroom with toys, crayons, and a little table and chair so she and Stephen could spend quality time together. He even ate dinner with her at his little table. But one day Stephen decided he needed a little more attention. He picked up her red lipstick and in no time had drawn designs all over the new cream-colored carpet!

like when you've had the flu and have been lying around in your sloppiest sweats looking crummy. The first day that you actually get dressed you feel like a million bucks. The same goes for bedrest. You also want to vary your daily outfits to help you differentiate one day from the next (they tend to start to blur together). Dress for your husband, too. He's the one who's going to see you the most. And even though he would be the first to say he loves you no matter what you look like, don't buy it. *You* have to like what you see when you look in the mirror—you don't want to lose a sense of who you are. We don't mean that you should be wearing scarves, beaded necklaces, or black leather boots while lying in bed, but you should just be aware of the situation—try to maintain some sort of personal style.

Think about your options. Now's probably not the time to rush out (or have someone rush out for you) to buy dazzling new clothes. What are you most comfortable in? Move those to the front of your closet so you can slip them on every morning without a second thought. For Cherie they were basics (actually Belly Basics). She had leggings in four colors: black, charcoal, navy, and brown, and tunics in black and charcoal. In addition, she had two favorite button-down shirts—one in denim and the other in red flannel. She looked different each day, and more important, she didn't look like she was sick in bed.

Getting dressed

Let's start at the very foundation—comfortable underclothes are key.

Underwear. Cotton is a must. Don't throw in the towel completely and buy dorky large briefs with flowers all over them, but at least make sure your underwear is big enough so that it doesn't bother you (refer to Chapter 3, "Closet Shopping").

Bra. It is tempting to want to eliminate a bra from your life. Don't. Your boobs are larger than ever and need a comfortable home. And just

because you're in bed all day, your bra shouldn't be any less supportive, either. The big question is, do you wear the same bra you wore before, or

do you need a different kind? Well, one of the goals of bedrest is relaxation—a stress-free environment. A pinching bra with underwires and clasps is not exactly heaven on earth, to say the least. We suggest you switch to either a "sleep bra" or a sports bra. These are both less structured but will give you full support.

• A sleep bra. These are available in the lingerie department or a lingerie store. They're much less constructed than a regular bra, and the fabric is usually cotton. They make you feel like you're wearing nothing more than an undershirt but with everything set nicely in place. But don't be lulled into a false sense of security; they don't give you serious support—the type D's, E's, and F's (god bless you!) might need. Smaller-breasted women can take the concept one step further—think about taking a bodysuit that you no longer wear and cutting the snaps off (see Chapter 3) The result is a comfortable cotton/Lycra "bra."

• A sports bra. Meant for jogging and movement, they're intrinsically designed to provide the firm support many women crave when pregnant. Cherie normally wears an underwire, which is totally uncomfortable if you're lying down, so she bought a sports bra to give her the needed support without digging into her ribs every time she moved a muscle. (The good news is that you could definitely wear both these bras after your pregnancy.) If you plan to breast-feed (see Chapter 10), they'll come in handy; and once your body is back to normal, you'll use them around the house or at the gym, so it's money well spent.

Leggings. A complete godsend to women on bedrest! The right cotton/Lycra leggings (the kind with either a very loose waistband or no elastic at all) can feel as comfortable as a pair of pajama bottoms. You can throw basically any kind of shirt over them without looking messy. Think about wearing a top that's the same color as the leggings for a slimming effect if you're having visitors.

Pull-on pants. If you've got a pull-on pant (elastic waist) that feels comfortable on you, whether it be wide leg, slim leg, or anywhere in between, wear it. Remember, comfort is the name of the game (as you know, we aren't the biggest advocates of full pants on pregnant women, but there are exceptions—bedrest is one). Just be wary of fabrics that wrinkle easily.

Shorts. If you are on bedrest in the heat of the summer, shorts are your best bet. The key is to find the ones that feel the most comfortable to you. We prefer the look and feel of bike shorts for a myriad of reasons. The Lycra portion of the fabric helps them feel supportive, and the cotton allows them to breath. They don't get wrinkled, and

Think about picking up some elastic-waist men's pajamas bottoms (large or extra-large) in classic stripe patterns or crisp solids. These can look chic with a white T-shirt.

some, like our own Belly Basics bike short, do not have a tight elastic waistband. Just remember to wear them with a T-shirt that's long enough to cover your thighs and butt (you don't want to scare away the UPS man).

Gym shorts or boxers are great, too. Yours (or, more likely, your husband's) might fit throughout a good part of your pregnancy, if not the whole way. Both of these can be used as

"fill-ins" when you're not expecting visitors. When your belly is still small and looks more like a pouch than anything else, boxers or gym shorts are a perfect way to expand your wardrobe. As your belly grows, you can fold the waistband comfortably under your tummy. Toward the end of your pregnancy, boxers and gym shorts aren't going to fit over your belly at all

Make sure you have something to do other than watching TV (a big time waster). Choose a project you can work on for a few hours each day—knitting booties, perhaps? No, really, if it strikes your fancy, go for it. Or if you have something that needs to get done, do it. Cherie's friend Lisa, a lawyer on bedrest with twins, decorated her entire babies' room using nothing more than a telephone, a pad, and a pencil.

and will look totally sloppy hanging down around your crotch—save these for real "off days," even though we know you'll be tempted to put them on daily. (You might even be tempted to leave them on for bedtime). Give them a rest—the "grumpy old man" look isn't the best for your self-esteem.

Shirts. The rule is, if it feels comfortable, toss it on. But it *must* cover your belly to look presentable. That means you shouldn't be lounging around in your old T-shirts if they don't cover your belly. Wear tops that hang well on your growing tummy. The shirts will probably end up coming out of your husband's closet. Pick out some of his softest, easiest-to-wear shirts and integrate them with your own favorites. T-shirts, oversized sweatshirts, tunics, and button-front shirts all work perfectly well. A magazine

If the doc says it's okay, do stretches and leg and arm exercises in bed. Giving your arms a workout and making your legs feel somewhat useful is not only good for the obvious reasons, but it will also help you sleep better. Inactivity can cause sleep difficulties.

beauty editor named Diane recently called us, frantic. She had been on bedrest for five months and had just hung up from her husband, Neil. They had their usual conversation, at the end of which he added, "Would you mind if Todd [his partner] comes over after work today to say hi and maybe have a beer . . . and do you think you could, uhh, put on some, you know . . . normal clothes?" Wow. Was it really that bad? She looked down at what she was wearing. It was what she wore practically every day: sweatpants that tied under her eighth-month belly and a ratty old T-shirt that clung to her bulging midsection. That's when she picked up the phone and called us. Diane explained that it simply hadn't occurred to her to buy maternity clothes since she had been on bedrest for so long. Why not just make do? But when Neil called it was like a lightbulb went on in her head: Why *shouldn't* she dress normally? We messengered over two Survival Kits. Diane's thank-you note read like this:

> You totally saved me! You changed my outlook on my entire pregnancy. I now know that I can be comfortable and presentable. What a concept. I even blow-dry my hair on occasion and put on a little mascara in the morning now. I know no one but my husband (and my close friends) will probably see me, but honestly I feel like a whole different person.

• Denim or flannel shirt. A denim shirt always looks good, it doesn't wrinkle easily, and usually your husband's will fit just fine (while we love crisp cotton men's shirts on pregnant women, this type of shirt tends to get very wrinkled). It looks good with leggings and with virtually any pant you decide to put on. A corduroy or velvet shirt will also work on bedrest (hey, you never know when you might need to dress up).

• Layering. A great idea. Think about layering T-shirts or long-sleeved cotton shirts under whatever you're wearing. Because you'll tend to get cold frequently now that you're not utilizing much energy, this is a good habit to get into. Start your morning with layers. When you get hot you can remove one layer without having to get up and change your shirt. Wear your denim or flannel shirts unbuttoned over a T-shirt or tunic top—just make sure the underneath layer isn't hanging out of the bottom. Yuck!

Dresses. If you are strictly confined to your bed, then dresses are pretty silly. But if you are allowed to spend the day on the couch and are expecting friends, a dress is a terrific option. Especially in the summer when you don't even need to wear hose, a cotton dress is perfectly comfortable. Recently Jody went to visit her old high school friend Ricci. Her definition of

bedrest was more like house arrest. As long as she was at home and sitting most of time, she was safe. She was allowed to take showers, answer the door, go into the kitchen, etc. Jody rang the doorbell expecting to find her fed-up, somewhat sloppy friend on the other side. To her pleasant surprise, she was greeted by Ricci, who was wearing our black Belly Basics dress and black opaque hose, looking terrific.

Bedrest is something that can't be avoided. Really. You've got to make the best of it. Before you know it, it will be but a distant memory in your harried, crazy, kid-filled life. Use this special time for yourself. Do something exotic like learn French. Catch up with friends whom you wish you'd stayed in better contact with. Rent movies you've always wanted to see but your husband has no interest in (in our houses, this list is endless). You're not the first person ever to go through this, nor will you be the last. We know that misery loves company, and believe us, you've got it! Get comfortable in your bed and settle in for the journey.

> Make a little effort and, for gosh sakes, put on some blush and mascara and run a comb through your hair. This will make you feel better about yourself, not to mention make your husband just a little happier.

More words of wisdom:

• Don't plan on spending your day "under cover." This sounds silly, but it's actually one of the most important bits of advice we could give you. Bedrest doesn't mean *in* bed; *on* bed is more like it. After you get dressed in the morning, have someone (you may not even be allowed) make your bed or at least straighten it out for you. Lie on top of your blanket. If your doctor allows it, try to make it to the couch for the bulk of your day.

• Eat healthy food. Don't eat junk because it's convenient or, worse yet, out of sheer boredom. Junk food will make you lethargic (the last thing you need) and fat. We're not talking pregnant fat, we're talking fat, fat, fat. Picture a pregnant woman lying in bed stuffing *Cheese Doodles* in her mouth. Not a lovely image. Surround yourself with things like carrots, rice cakes, and fruit as your "boredom snacks" and save the goodies for dessert.

• Say yes to an extra pair of hands to help you with meals, run to the grocery store, or just keep you company. For Cherie, it was her parents. They actually moved in for a few weeks and were indispensable. They not only helped keep her spirits up during the day, but they helped take care of her son. Her mom even made dinner for the entire family. What a luxury.

• If the weather is beautiful (and you're looking out the window, bumming out, wishing it were raining instead), sit outside in the shade for an hour or two, if the doctor will allow. Francesca, the woman who runs our favorite coffee bar around the corner from our office, was on bedrest for a few months (we were almost as bummed as she was—the coffee was horrendous during her absence). She had her husband buy a lawn chair that barely squeezed onto her Manhattan terrace (really a fire escape, but that's just semantics) so she could get a little fresh air.

• Keep in mind that once the baby comes, you'll actually be yearning for days like this . . . days you probably won't see again for at least twenty years.

Hit the road:
Travel

Travel. Travel. Travel. As much as you can. It doesn't matter where you go. Just go—a lot—before the baby comes. Once you become a parent, even a simple weekend at the beach becomes more complicated than you ever could've imagined. Packing takes on a whole new meaning. It means not only thinking through your wardrobe, but remembering to include diapers, wipes, formula, extra bottles, baby food, car seats, strollers, not to mention pack 'n' plays, undershirts, pjs, socks, and toys. Whew. So let's concentrate on the present and plan some trips. We'll tell you what to take when you go. We both love to travel and really lived it up during our first pregnancies. We were prepared for everything, yet we were never caught lugging a too-heavy suitcase.

The first thing you need to know when preparing for a trip is that you don't have to take every single thing that fits, even though the temptation is there. You think, Well, I did buy these things for my pregnancy, I might as well take them with me—they'll serve no purpose sitting at home in my closet. While this thinking is logical, it'll make for an extremely heavy suitcase, not to mention an annoying session of "what to wear" when you should be off frolicking with your husband.

Focus on the core pieces, the ones that you wear day in and day out. If you've followed our advice throughout this book, your core pieces will all be the same color (hopefully black or neutral). If you have three or four pieces that you can't live without, that's more than enough for a weekend jaunt. And, with the addition of a few extra pieces, enough for an entire week.

To make it easy to plan, take a step back and look at your needs. In the broadest sense, we have city travel and country travel. If you really stop to analyze where you're going, it should fit into one of these two areas.

City travel

By this we mean any trip that takes you someplace where you'll be in a city environment. It doesn't necessarily have to be an actual city. Many times while she was pregnant, Jody and David went "home" to suburban Michigan. Although her hometown is a far cry from a city, Jody packed a more urban selection of clothes. Her plans included seeing friends, shopping with her mom, going to lunch with her dad, and eating dinners out at trendy restaurants with her brother and sister-in-law. Here's what to pack:

Essentials: leggings, tunic, and dress

Accessories: opaque hose, flat loafers, higher (dressier) shoes, a variety of necklaces, scarves, a sweater to wear around your shoulders, a blazer (think of your blazer as an accessory), and perhaps a tailored men's shirt (could be one of your husband's).

Airplane trips are very dehydrating, so take along a bottle of water. Nothing is more annoying—to you or the flight attendant—than continually asking for refills of H_2O in your little airplane cup.

Country travel

Don't just think cows, farms, and bumpy back roads. Country means someplace where you won't have to dress for anything. Like visiting a place where, if you weren't pregnant, you'd spend the entire time in jeans, shorts, sweatshirts, or swimsuits. This would include going to the beach, checking out the fall foliage, taking a "kid" trip with your older child. While days are usually spent outdoors and active, nights can be a little more dressy. Cherie's favorite weekend getaway is to go antiquing—meandering in and out of shops in a small, out-of-the-way town. Daniel planned a few of these perfect short trips during both pregnancies (it was in his best interests to keep her happy).

Packing was a cinch—there was no need to get dressed up.

Here's what you'll need:

Essentials: leggings (bike shorts in summer), a big sweater or T-shirt, a tunic, a button-down cotton shirt or a denim shirt, and a swimsuit (if necessary).

Accessories: comfortable shoes (or gym shoes), a pair of shoes that are slightly dressier for the evening (e.g., sandals in summer, or boots in winter), and either one scarf or one great necklace.

Now, the nitty gritty: "How on earth can I go away for four days with just four pieces?"

Easily. We planned all of our trips this way, and in fact, still do. The key? Take only your essentials and wear them in different ways at different times of the day. For example, you'll wear the leggings while you're traveling. Pair them with anything from your basic tunic to a cotton sweater or a big flannel shirt. If you're stopping somewhere on the way or going directly out, wear them with a matching tunic. Upon arrival, you'll continue to wear them, but in different ways. Throw on one of your husband's white shirts when you get to your hotel room. Whether you're sightseeing in Paris, antiquing in Vermont, or spending the day at an amusement park, leggings are the call. Add a scarf if you need to. The core pieces that you wear during the day will afford you a completely different option at night. The thread that ties these pieces together is your shoes and accessories. The same leggings and tunic that work with a pair of comfortable shoes during the day will be just right for the finest restaurant—just wear a shoe that's more fashionable, maybe something that has a higher heel. If you really want to dress it up, tie a classic scarf around your neck or wear a pearl necklace. Last summer, well into her eighth month, Jody and David rented a house with another family for a long July 4th weekend at the beach. She packed her swimsuit, bike shorts, a short-sleeved tunic, a few big T-shirts, and a simple cotton/Lycra dress. For going out to breakfast or taking her eighteen-month-old for a walk

on the beach, bike shorts and a T-shirt were fine. Swimsuit and dress for the beach. Her days were set. To go to dinner at night, she slipped on bike shorts and the short-sleeve tunic with flat sandals. She wore her dress to a slightly fancier restaurant. She actually had an easier time getting dressed than her friend Libby, who was busy sifting through a million options she had thrown into her suitcase.

Travel doesn't have to be far or expensive to be fun. It's the best way to spend quality time with your husband. Just closely follow our detailed packing instructions. Check with your ob/gyn first, then grab your suitcase, a good book, a big bottle of water, and get outta here.

> Keep the bathroom factor in mind when planning your trip. If you're taking an airplane, don't even think of booking the window seat. If you're driving a car, keep in mind that you'll be making frequent pit stops. Remember to build extra time into your plans.

So where's the instruction book?

After

The past few days have been a whirlwind, exciting beyond your wildest imagination. Going into labor, getting through delivery, recuperating (if you call it that) at the hospital while trying to learn *anything* about your wee one. Then, bringing him home and making sure he's comfortable in his new digs. This tiny little baby is occupying your every thought and every waking moment. Your entire being centers around him.

But what about you? You're sore, exhausted, and unshowered (a shower is a luxury these days), wearing at best a big T-shirt and sweatpants. And you surely don't have the luxury of being alone to even revel in your new family. Oh, no. Your house is filled with well-meaning relatives and friends who have come to see the new addition. Life around you is going full speed, and, believe it or not, you've got to get dressed for it.

When Stephen was an infant, Cherie felt guilty every time she went to blow her hair. When he was up, she felt like she should be with him, not her hair dryer. When he was sleeping, she felt she should be doing some-

When you pack your bag for the hospital, you're usually so busy concentrating on the endless list of little things you'll need for delivery that it's easy to forget the big picture—like the fact that when you leave the hospital you're not going to be pregnant anymore. The maternity clothes that you wore to the hospital probably won't work for you when you leave, with baby in your arms rather than in your belly. Remember to toss in a pair of leggings and a big shirt or even a simple cotton dress.

thing baby related, like preparing bottles, washing his clothes or, god knows, writing thank-you notes. It's as if when the baby pops

out, the guilt pops in. But tending to some of your own needs *is* important—if you feel good, your baby will feel just a little better, too. Infants are very in tune with the vibes their parents give off. Allow yourself a sufficient amount of time during the morning to take a shower (it's okay if the baby cries for a few minutes while you're in there), fix your hair, and get dressed (and we mean *dressed*— sweat-pants don't count).

Ah . . . getting dressed. It sounds easier than it is. Your first impulse is probably to grab your favorite maternity essentials out of months of habit. Then, immediately, you remember that you're not pregnant anymore. So you reach for your pre-pregnancy favorites. But it's not the right time for these either. Foiled again. Most of your maternity clothes are no longer appropriate, nor do you really feel like wearing them (on the contrary, you probably feel like burning them). You're not yet ready for your old favorites because, besides the fact that you still have baby weight to deal with, your bone structure has temporarily changed, too. After Cherie had become frustrated with her own situation, her doctor patiently explained at her post-baby checkup that a woman's whole pelvic area shifts around during pregnancy and that it takes time for everything to "settle back in." Great.

This means different things for different people. It could take weeks, months, or maybe even a year for your body to look the way it did before. Here's where we come in. There are plenty of things that you can wear during this "hiatus" without looking like you're all belly. Heaven forbid someone should ask you when you're due! This happened to our friend Wendy four months after she had her baby. Embarrassed, she quietly answered, "I'm not pregnant," to which the stranger reacted with visible shock. Certainly Wendy

looked pregnant—her belly hadn't totally gone back to pre-pregnancy size, and her clothes looked like maternity duds. What was the stranger to think?

What to wear

Remember your favorites when you were five or six months pregnant? Try. Your belly is about the size it was then (though we know it hurts to admit it). Certain items are essentials for this post-pregnancy time.

Leggings. Our number-one piece of clothing (surely you guessed it by now). Immediately after the baby is born, you should continue to wear your maternity leggings. They'll be the

If you've had a C-section, you'll find that leggings with a nonelastic waistband are a must. Anything else will irritate your sore belly. Our friend Patricia not only wore our Belly Basics leggings during the daytime, but she got herself another pair to sleep in at night. She found them to be the best and most comfortable way to dress while she recovered.

most comfortable. After you begin to lose some baby weight, you'll be ready to switch back to regular leggings.

Boxer shorts. They are the perfect thing to wear around the house. Comfortable, washable, and easy, they won't constrain your healing body. Even in the middle of winter, Jody slept in a soft flannel pair. Toss on a big T-shirt or sweatshirt with them. Something else you should try are men's boxer "briefs" (Calvin was the originator, but now you can find them everywhere). They look like a long version of regular men's underwear, but the twist is that they are the length of boxers. You can get them in the men's underwear department of any store. Jody wore David's a lot for the first few weeks. Because they were solid black or heather gray, they didn't look like men's underwear when she wore them with a big T-shirt.

Pants with a drawstring waist. They hide your tummy nicely while giving you some extra room all around.

Elastic-waist pants that contain Lycra. They'll stretch with you. Try your riding-style pants or stretchy boot-leg pants. They may not look quite the way you had hoped, but worn with a big top they'll camouflage your trouble areas.

A long knit skirt. It's comfortable, you don't have to wear hosiery with it, and it usually has an elastic waistband, which should fit comfortably on your tummy. A loose cotton button-down shirt looks great with a long skirt. Go casual with flat sandals or mules, or dress it up slightly with low heels or boots.

And what to wear on top?

If you've decided to breast-feed, there are certain issues to think about. Since you're going to be opening your shirt at least eight to ten times each day, make it as easy for yourself as possible. The first two options are perfect for you. If you're not planning to breast-feed, all of the following suggestions work equally well.

A button-front shirt. At this point you should be able to fit into some of your normal pre-pregnancy shirts. It's a welcome relief when suddenly the shirts that stopped fitting months ago magically fit again. But everyone's body is different—you might feel more comfortable in your husband's or wearing your maternity shirts for a while longer. We both lived in our husband's button-front shirts throughout the "feeding frenzy" of the first month or two.

Big T-shirts or sweaters. Sometimes it's more comfortable (and less obvious) to lift up a sweater than to unbutton a shirt. The weather, oddly enough, factors into it. When it's cold, you don't want to expose any more skin than necessary, and T-shirts or sweaters are great (button-front shirts are better when it's warm).

Big knit maternity tops. A good rule of thumb? Wear your favorite solid tunic if—and only if—the cut is simple and it looks like a regular top. Maternity clothes, if they are designed properly, should be able to be worn after the baby is born. The key is the fabric and the construction: It must be soft and drapey to work. If it's a woven item like a blazer, jacket,

148
....
after

You can buy tops designed especially for breast-feeding. The one catch is that they aren't the most happening clothes in the world (you've just gone through nine long months of having to wear "specially designed" clothes—why prolong it?). Our advice? Stay clear of them unless you plan to breast-feed for a year or longer.

or constructed pants, leave it in the back of your closet until the next go-around. It will look stiff, oversized and, in a word, ridiculous on you now.

Dresses. One of the most comfortable items to wear post-baby is a dress. You can wear either your favorite knit maternity dress or one of the fuller dresses you wore at the beginning of your pregnancy. A dress is great because not only is it comfortable for your entire body, but it hides your post-baby belly exceptionally well. It's very forgiving for your first few weeks of motherhood. Just don't expect to breast-feed

with it on unless it has a button front. But if you leave your baby at home for an hour or two, it's perfect. Jody wore her black Belly Basics dress four days after she came home from the hospital when David insisted that they go out for dinner. She literally hadn't left the house since the hospital (it's easy to become a bit of a shut-in). Anyway, she agreed to go, wrapping a black sweater around her newly returning waist to give it some definition. The dress looked terrific (however, she missed her new baby girl terribly and was ready to return home after appetizers).

Bras. Every woman feels differently about the type of bra she chooses for breast-feeding. Some women run right out and pick up a nursing bra and stick with it the whole time. Others, like Jody, use a front-closure bra not specifically designed for nursing. Hers was actually her mom's. She hadn't given the bra subject any thought until *bam*—her boobs filled up and all her bras were too snug. Her mom, in from Michigan for the week, had a few bras with her. They were perfect. A front-closure bra not necessarily designed for breast-feeding can be just as convenient as a nursing bra. It's really a matter of how much money you want to invest, how long you plan to

Not only do button-front shirts allow for easy access to baby's next meal, but the chest pockets will be surprisingly helpful to you. Cherie used this pocket as a place to arm herself with a spare pacifier, so she was always ready for action. And Jody stored her vitamin E oil there so she'd have it to use after every feeding on her cracked nipples (sounds lovely, doesn't it?). By the way, vitamin E oil is great for sore nipples. It heals them quicker than everything else we've tried. Apply it in its true liquid form (you can either pick up a bottle of vitamin E oil or buy the caplets and break them open). Use it after every feeding, but remember to wipe any remainder off before your baby latches back on.

You think your chest went through some major changes during your pregnancy? You ain't seen nothing yet. Whether you choose to breast-feed or not, your breasts are going to fill up with milk. What's still mind-boggling to us is how your body knows just what to do. Your baby is out, and three or four days later, like clockwork, your breasts fill up. The next thing you know, you've got milk seeping from your nipples. Unbelievable. Here are some tips for dealing with this:

• If you're not going to breast-feed, you've got to wear something tight to relieve the pain and to stop the milk production as quickly as you can. The best solution we've heard of is to wear a workout bra. This binds your chest tightly as you become engorged. You're going to want to sleep in it, too. Engorged breasts can be pretty painful. If you get really uncomfortable, put ice packs directly onto them. (Hint: Warm water makes the milk flow, so although you might be tempted, try not to take a really hot shower.)

• If you are going to breast-feed, the first thing you have to do is pick up some disposable breast pads, which are available at every drugstore—you can send your husband to pick them up while he's out getting a breast pump, rubbing alcohol, baby lotion, and all the other things you thought you had but now realize you don't. For the first few months of breast-feeding, you'll need to put these pads in your bra to soak up the leaks. If you plan to breast-feed for a long time, think about cloth pads—better for the environment and cheaper in the long run. They are meant to be tossed into the washing machine each day with the baby's laundry.

breast-feed, and what makes you the most comfortable. Cherie bought a nursing bra but didn't love its construction. She bought it before the baby was even born after some "seasoned" moms convinced her that it was a must-have. Not really knowing what to look for, she ended up with one where the flaps snapped close. The snaps were a pain in the neck. Half the time she ended up pulling the whole side of the bra up over her boob. Our only advice? Comfort should be your key criterion in choosing your post-baby bra.

Did someone say "party"?

Believe it or not, there are some dressy occasions that tend to come up immediately following the birth of your baby. We know it's weird. You've just had a baby and you're utterly exhausted. You can barely sit down even with the aid of a rubber donut, you can't move any faster than a slow walk, and you're forced to either entertain, go out for a fancy dinner, or, in some cases, welcome your entire circle of friends, family, and neighbors into your home for a party. You've actually got to look good. Hang in there. *It is* possible. You've just got to make it easy for yourself. You've got to choose something that's not only comfortable for your sore bottom, but that will cover your still-bulging tummy without making you look pregnant. (Oh, is that all?)

These occasions may include: a bris, a christening, a birthday, or a holiday celebration. Sometimes they can creep up on you without warning—Cherie was inundated with a string of events only weeks after Jonathan was born. First, the bris. Then Stephen's third birthday celebration (Jonathan was born within days of Stephen's birthday). This ended up being a big deal because everyone

If you can arrange to have your mom or a good friend watch the baby, treat yourself to a much needed evening out. A simple thing like this, something you've probably taken for granted until now, will not be so easy later when all of your "helping hands" are not as available.

wanted to see the new addition. And a mere two days later, it was time for her own birthday celebration (January is a big month in the Serota home). Talk about an impending wardrobe crisis! Here's how to tackle it:

• Wait until one day prior to pick out your outfit. Each and every day your belly will go down significantly, so wait as long as you can.

• Take a look in your closet for any elastic-waist nonmaternity skirts or pants. If you can find any that fit, you're in luck (otherwise, pull out your most inocuous, least offensive basic maternity dress and call it a day).

• Look for a big shirt (either a sweater, a blouse, or a tunic) that you can wear untucked. If you can find a blazer that ties it all together, you'll be set.

For Stephen's birthday party Cherie wore black wide-leg, elastic-waist pants with a button-down shirt (untucked), pearls, and suede loafers. For her own birthday celebration with Daniel (two days later), she chose a long black knit skirt, a soft, drapey silk knit sweater, and an unconstructed blazer to wear to their favorite restaurant. It seemed appropriate for the way she felt (like a real grown-up) now that she had a family of four. She didn't feel quite as sophisticated as she looked, though, when she whipped out her floral throw pillow to sit on at the restaurant as the maître d' stood silently beside her.

When Jody had her son's bris last summer, she wore a short, pleated elastic-waist skirt with a sleeveless turtleneck (she borrowed the sweater from her mom, who's a few sizes bigger than she is). To cover the clingy knit sweater, she wore a blazer, unbuttoned. She looked almost like her regular self again. Only she knew that the skirt had an elastic waist and her mom's shirt was camouflaging the remnants of her bulging belly.

Whether you have a good reason to get

We received a letter from a woman named Melanie, an accountant in North Carolina. She told us that after one solid hour of trying to put together an outfit for her daughter's christening, she finally reached for her Belly Basics. She wore our skirt and long-sleeved tunic with a long gabardine pinstripe vest and looked terrific. We know the details because she actually sent us a photo!

dressed or not, try to give it your all. Post-baby is a very stressful time, and wearing clothes that make you feel like a person is one positive step toward regaining a sense of normalcy in your life. We suggest trying on different pieces from your pre-pregnancy wardrobe on a continual basis. What you think won't fit you just might. You'll be too limiting in your selections if you don't periodically check through everything. With each passing day, your body will get smaller (from losing excess water weight

alone). And before you know it, getting dressed will no longer be an ordeal. One day you're going to try on your jeans and they're actually going to fit—and this will all be but a distant memory. We promise.

Resource Guide

Stores

Bloomingdale's	800/555-SHOP
Nordstrom	888/HOSE 2 GO
Loehmann's	718/409-2000
Marshalls	800/MARSHALLS
The Limited	800/756-4449
Express	614/479-4031
Kmart	800/63 KMART
The Gap	800/GAP STYLE
Banana Republic	888/277-8953
Mom's Night Out	212/744-6667

Catalogues

Motherwear	800/950-2500
Bloomingdale's-By-Mail	800/777-0000
Garnet Hill	800/622-6216
J.Crew	800/562-0258
Nordstrom Direct	800/285-5800

Manufacturers

Belly Basics	800/4 9 MONTHS
Japanese Weekend	800/808-0555
Eileen Fisher	800/345-3362
Emanuel	212/683-1000
Fitigues	800/235-9005
Joan Vass	888/987-1306
C.P. Shades	212/966-5467
Norma Kamali	212/957-9797